DIVINE
ENCOUNTER

CELEBRATING
GOD'S CALENDAR.
CELESTIAL CLUES.
CULMINATION OF CREATION.

ROD PARSLEY

RESUL**t**S
PUBLISHING

Columbus, Ohio

Divine Encounter

ISBN: 978-0-9907578-2-5
Copyright © 2015 by Rod Parsley

Published by:
Results Publishing
P.O. Box 100
Columbus, Ohio 43216-0100 USA

CONTENTS

DEDICATION

I can think of no greater person to whom I could dedicate this work than Senior Elder Bill Canfield. A man of immense integrity, remarkable wisdom, and superior intellect. A true theologian and a prolific author. A preacher of the gospel and a teacher of the Word. A man who is uncompromising in his convictions, undeniable in his character, unparalleled in his counsel, and unmatched in his commitment to seeing the Kingdom of God established in these culminating days.

For thirty-two years, he has stood by my side through every trial and every triumph. We have cried together, prayed together, and rejoiced together. Never wavering or wandering, he remains solid, steadfast, and strong. His faithfulness and dedication to the body of Christ, to the ministries of World Harvest Church, to the Parsley family, and to me, personally, is something only comparable to when Aaron and Hur held up the arms of Moses.

My pastor and mentor, Dr. Lester Sumrall, once told me, "Rod, if you leave this earth with two or three true friends, you've died a rich man." Well, now that Dr. Sumrall has gone on to receive his eternal reward, that pastoral vacancy has been filled by not only an admired and respected mentor, but by one of those very few, true friends.

So, I thank you, Elder Canfield, for being an accelerator of the vision. I thank you for being the pastor of my old age. But most of all, I thank you for being that which God calls *merea*–companion, advisor, and friend.

Understanding the *Feasts* of Israel

2 SEASONS, 3 DIVISIONS, 7 FEASTS

Spring

Former/Early Rain - *Historically Fulfilled Feasts*

Fall

Latter Rain - *Historically Unfulfilled Feasts*

Passover	Pentecost	Tabernacles
1 Feast of Passover	**4** Feast of Weeks/Pentecost	**5** Feast of Trumpets
2 Feast of Unleavened Bread		**6** Feast of Day of Atonement
3 Feast of First Fruits		**7** Feast of Tabernacles

Corresponding Hebrew (Lunar) Calendar Months

Nisan	Iyar	Sivan	Tishrei
(March - April)	*(April - May)*	*(May - June)*	*(September - October)*

Jewish Month	Approximate Secular Date	This Month's Special Dates
Nisan *(NEE-sahn)*	March - April	Passover
Iyar *(EE-yahr)*	April - May	Lag B'Omer *(lagh-BO-mer)*
Sivan *(see-VAHN)*	May - June	Shavuot *(sha-voo-OHT)*
Tammuz *(tam-MOOZ)*	June - July	
Av *(ahv)*	July - August	Tisha B'Av *(tish-ah-BHAV)*
Elul *(el-OOL)*	August - September	
Tishrei *(tish-RAY)*	September - October	The High Holidays (Rosh Hashanah *[rahsh hah-SHAH-nah]* and Yom Kippur *[yohm kee-POOR]*), Sukkot *(soo-kote)*, Shemini Atzeret *(SH-MEE-nee aht-ZEH-reht)*, and Simchat Torah *(SEEM-kaht TOH-rah)*
Cheshvan *(KESH-vahn)*	October - November	
Kislev *(KEES-lev)*	November - December	Hanukkah
Tevet *(teh-VEHT)*	December - January	Conclusion of Hanukkah
Shevat *(shuh-VAHT)*	January - February	Tu B'Shvat *(too bee-shuh-VAHT)*
Adar I *(uh-DAHR)*	February - March	Purim *(poo-REEM)*

Wisdom of the Rabbis

One fundamental criterion
of a life well lived is love of life.
It is terribly important, therefore,
to enjoy life as it goes along.
Joy cannot be postponed.
Life is of infinite value.

~ Rabbi Irving Greenberg

INTRODUCTION

I will forever remember making my inaugural visit to the nation of Israel and touring the ancient city of Jerusalem. It was the first time I had truly experienced the revelation of my Jewish roots and the last time I would ever view my spiritual heritage – and even the Bible – in the same way I had before. I believe that we Christians are often quick to forget that our Lord and Savior, from whom we receive our divine genealogy, was a Jew. How, then, can we possibly understand the gospel if we don't understand the Hebrew culture, practices, and traditions upon which our faith was founded – those customs that the very Son of God Himself observed and practiced? In fact, how can we truly understand Jesus Christ Himself?

I vividly recall visiting the place where this same Jesus walked the crusty surface of this peopled planet. Rich with history, full of mysterious and exceptional beauty, Jerusalem is where I saw the Bible come alive in living color. I remember one evening in particular I was riding in a little white van with my pastor and mentor, Dr. Lester Sumrall. We were traveling from Jericho to Jerusalem. As we bounced and rocked on the uneven cobblestones beneath us, I thought, "This is one of the very streets trod by my precious Lord Himself. It was here that John the Baptist said, *'There cometh one mightier than I after me, the latchet of whose shoes I am not worthy to stoop down and unloose'* (Mark 1:7). It was upon these roads that the mighty prophet Elijah carried his mantle" (2 Kings 2:13).

How could I ever adequately describe the feeling of being in such a place? This is where the King of Glory performed the miracles that I'd read about. Where the Prince of Peace was crucified just as the songs I had sung so often described. Where Jesus Christ had died and risen again, just as I had preached so many times.

As I contemplated that sacred, ageless city, I felt tears begin to stream down my face, warming my cheeks. No sooner had I wiped them away and begun to consider some of the other biblical events that had occurred in that historic setting than we rounded a corner. There it was! The City of God! I had barely a breath left in me to breathe. The sun was ablaze in mellow saffron, golden orange, and fiery red as it began to take its final plunge into the Mediterranean, there to be extinguished for another night. She gave forth her final and most colorful beams, shining and shimmering like a diamond on a velvet couch. There, in the distance, arose the capital and center of our Father's most hallowed land. O Jerusalem, Jerusalem! I was on that evening, and forever, changed. I have not been the same since.

★

That first experience in Jerusalem has led directly to this book. It is the deepest desire of my heart that those who read these pages experience the same awestruck wonder and intimate connection to the City of God and our Hebrew roots as I did on that first memorable trip to the earthly home of our God and King. I pray that these pages inspire curiosity, provoke thought, quell speculation, and – most importantly – bridge the gap between our modern-day religiosity and the time-honored conventions of ages past. Let us with one hand reach back to the discarded values that have dethroned principalities and powers in the past and with the other hand reach forward to the purpose, promise, and power of a new generation.

There is another reason I have written this book, and I want to state it boldly. The Bible declares in John 4:23, "The hour is coming, and now is, when the true worshipers will worship the Father in spirit and truth; for the Father is seeking such to worship Him" (NKJV).

I believe many people today are weary of going through the motions and are saying, "Lord, I desire to know You in a greater dimension, in a greater glory, in a greater passion." A remnant are crying out to God and saying, "Lord, I'm not satisfied with church as usual. I want Your glory!" I hope you're among these hungry ones. There are always deeper depths and higher heights available. There are always greater anointings to be had. There is always a more powerful experience possible in the things of God.

The Bible declares that when the farmer went forth to sow, some seed fell on good ground, some on thorny ground, and some on stony ground. Some also fell by the wayside. Yet some fell on the good ground and brought forth a harvest thirtyfold, sixtyfold, and one hundredfold beyond what was planted (Mark 4:3-8). Tragically, I believe many in today's church are satisfied with having only a thirtyfold revelation of the Abba of Jesus.

There are different dimensions in God. This can be illustrated by the courts of the Hebrew Temple. There is an outer court, there is an inner court, and there is the innermost place of the Holy of Holies, where God dwells in manifest glory. This three-tiered progression is everywhere in Scripture. There are Father, Son, and Holy Ghost. We speak of faith, hope, and love. We undergo water baptism, Spirit baptism, and fire baptism. There are always new heights and new depths we have yet to reach, and they are often revealed in a set of three. We cannot escape the power of three in God's Word. David received his first anointing to fight the bear. He acquired his second anointing to rule Judah. He gained his third anointing to rule Israel. Joseph got his first coat from his father. He received his second coat from Potiphar and his third coat from Pharaoh.

Remember Ruth? She was getting the leftovers of the field. That's thirtyfold. Boaz saw her and put her in the fruitful part of the field. That's sixtyfold. Then she married Boaz and received one hundredfold! It requires little effort to remain at the thirtyfold level. It's easy to settle and become comfortable. After all, the outer court is the most expansive portion of the Temple! A lot of folks dwell in the outer court because that's where all the fun is. Yet after a while we should grow weary of the outer court and yearn to go deeper. There should develop within us a dissatisfaction with simply going to church services and performing the minimum requirements of religious routine. Rather, there should arise within us a yearning to know Him, a hunger to abide in His glorious presence and to worship at His precious feet. This desire consumed Paul. In Philippians 3, he basically said,

> *Listen, I'm educated. I've been to the best schools. I've walked with the powerful and been among the elite. I've done all the religious rituals, and I've done them correctly. But I recognize that when it comes to God, none of the rudimentary obligations of religion accomplishes anything. I count it all as dung. Instead, I want to know Him. I desire to know Him in a very deep and everlasting way.*

This book is for those who, like Paul, want to know Jesus in a deeper way. Ever since my first visit to Jerusalem I have believed that we, as Christians, must come to understand the seasons of God and the feasts of God in order to fully understand what our Lord

Jesus accomplished for and provided to us. I invite you to plumb new depths, scale new heights, and explore new horizons with me. I desire for you to learn with me the calendar of God and the prescribed celebrations of God and thereby receive the tremendous revelations that God intends for those who keep His feasts. I believe your eyes are going to be opened, and you will see Jesus and your world in an entirely new way. This is what it means to abide in the calendar of God and to live in His times, His cycles, and His seasons of celebration and remembrance.

★

Before we begin our journey in these pages, I want to share a word of encouragement with you. We are going to be dealing with many Hebrew words that are likely unfamiliar to you. Have no fear! I'll do everything I can to make them as user-friendly as possible. Allow me to tell a story from my early life that I hope will calm some of your "I'm stepping into untested waters" nerves!

One of my earliest memories of reading as a child was lying down on the red-and-black shag carpet of my bedroom with a book my mother had purchased for me. Being a child of the sixties, I was fascinated by stories of war, so my mother bought for me a novel that was set in the barracks and foxholes of a World War II army platoon. Literacy was important to my parents, my mother in particular. She took every pain to instill in me a love for the written word. She knew that a story of combat, brotherhood, patriotism, and history was perfect for feeding my love of reading and my interest in the past.

I was so enthralled by the story in the novel and the "big words" that peppered its pages that I could not wait to read it aloud to my parents. I knew they were sure to delight in my newfound vocabulary and praise me for my growing intellect. The grand moment finally arrived after dinner one autumn evening at our avocado-colored kitchen table. (Remember, it was the sixties!) As I read with great conviction and confidence, I suddenly noticed that my parents were not praising me and congratulating me for my oratory as I had expected. Instead, they were grinning sheepishly and turning their heads, pretending to cough in order to cover their chuckles.

I was confused and flustered. I demanded to know why they were not more excited by their boy's brilliance. My mother, placing her hand gently on my shoulder and leaning down so her cheek touched mine, said with a whisper, "Son, it's pronounced 'colonel,' not 'colonial.'" My father, smiling from behind his coffee cup, also reassured me: "That's a good try, bud. A good try. Awful big words in there for a fella to learn."

I was disappointed, devastated even. To think that I had been pronouncing the word for a high-ranking officer in the army like a type of salad dressing was a horrible embarrassment. However, my parents took the time to explain that this was a common error and that the word "*colonel*" was actually a homonym – a word that sounded like another but had a different spelling or meaning. "Like a popcorn *kernel*. Colonel. Kernel. That's how you say it. Same pronunciation. Same way. It just doesn't mean the same thing," my mother explained. I was relieved to know that I was not as unintelligent as I felt at that moment, but that words we have never seen or do not use on a regular basis are often difficult to pronounce or understand.

I say this by way of assuring you that I have taken the liberty to provide the phonetic spelling and pronunciation of many words and phrases throughout this book, words that could easily become confusing and/or distracting. I certainly do not want anyone developing a reader's complex like I did with the colonel/colonial debacle. Oh, and by the way, my eight-year-old self wants to remind you that it is pronounced "antique" and not "an-ti-cue," another mistake I made at one of the Parsley family dinner readings.

❧   ❧   ❧

Wisdom of the Rabbis

*There is no man free like the one
who is involved with the study of Torah.*

~ Rabbi Yehoshuah ben Levi

*Torah is not an education,
it's a transformation.*

~ Rebbitzen Dena Weinberg

Chapter I

A BLESSING FOR READING GOD'S WORD

Birkat HaTorah
(Beer-KAHT Ha-TOH-rah)

A Blessing for the Learning of Torah[1]
Recited as part of the *Shacharit* (shah-khah-REET),
which is the morning service in the synagogues of the world.

———————

Blessed art Thou, Lord our God, King of the universe, who has sanctified us with His commandments and commanded us to engross ourselves with the words of Torah.

Please Lord, our God, sweeten the words of Your Torah in our mouths and in the mouths of all Your people Israel. May we and our offspring, and the offspring of Your people, the House of Israel, may we all, together, know Your Name and study Your Torah for the sake of fulfilling Your desire. Blessed are You, Lord, Who teaches Torah to His people Israel.

Blessed are You, Lord our God, King of the universe, Who chose us from all the nations and gave us the Torah. Blessed are You, Lord, Giver of the Torah.

May the Lord bless you and keep watch over you; May the Lord make His Presence enlighten you, and may He be kind to you; May the Lord bestow favor on you, and grant you peace.

———————

[1] The word *torah (TOH-rah)* literally means "teaching" or "instruction." Though the word is commonly used to describe the first five books of the Old Testament, it can also mean the whole of God's revelation to His people and thus can be used by both Christians and Jews as a term for God's word or truth.

❧ ❧ ❧

WISDOM OF THE RABBIS

There are no two hours alike. Every hour is unique and the only one given at the moment, exclusive and endlessly precious. Judaism teaches us to be attached to holiness in time; to learn how to consecrate sanctuaries that emerge from the magnificent stream of a year.

~ Rabbi Abraham Joshua Heschel

The command "you shall remain joyful" turns your rejoicing into a permanent trait of your personality, and the words "only joyful" mean that this joyfulness in your character will persist even under circumstances that would otherwise tend to cast a cloud over it. You will remain joyful in spite of everything, "only" joyful. Simchah, rejoicing, is the most sublime flower and fruit to open on the tree of life planted by the Law of God. In the same spirit, the joyfulness . . . is not restricted to festivals and festive gatherings but extends beyond the festive seasons and accompanies us back into everyday life, from the exuberance of the festive assemblies into the quiet privacy of our homes, and remains with us through all the vicissitudes of life.

~ Rabbi Samson Raphael Hirsch

❧ ❧ ❧

Chapter II

THE SEASONS OF OUR GOD

O ur God is a God of timing, a God of seasons, and a God of cycles. These truths leap from nearly every page of Scripture. In the Bible that I am using as I write these words, there are nearly 1,166 pages. Surprisingly, there are more than 800 verses in that Bible in which God declares that He is concerned with times, seasons, and cycles. That's almost one verse for every page! This is one of the most important truths we can know about our God. Yet it is more than a truth; it is an invitation. It is like the insight a husband gets into his wife's soul that helps him love her more deeply and fill her days with greater joy. It is knowledge that invites relationship; knowledge that issues a call. From the very beginning, God set in motion His times, cycles, and seasons. We see this as we read the words from Genesis that describe the creation of the heavens:

> "And God said, Let there be lights in the firmament of the heaven to divide the day from the night; and let them be for signs, and for seasons, and for days, and years: And let them be for lights in the firmament of the heaven to give light upon the earth: and it was so" (Genesis 1:14-15)

I read these words many times before I began to understand their deeper meaning. I read them as most of us do – as a description of the beginning of all we see in the sky. I mean, the verses mention day and night, seasons and years, and lights in the heavens. It all seemed pretty simple to me back then. There came a moment, though, when I began to understand that these words were not intended as a guide for stargazing. They were given to introduce us to the times and seasons by which God rules the world of men. You see, there is more in these verses than just astronomical information. There is a powerful revelation of how the heavenly bodies define God's holy seasons and festivals and the revelation of His glory we gain as we observe them. Let me share portions of this passage with you in some translations other than my trusty King James Version and perhaps you'll understand.

> **God's Word Translation:** "They will be signs and will mark religious festivals, days, and years."

> **The Amplified Bible:** "Let them be signs and tokens [of God's provident care]."

> **New International Version:** "Let them serve as signs to mark sacred times, and days and years."

Do you see it? There is a hidden meaning in the original Hebrew language. The Bible does not just say that the sun, moon, and stars will be for "signs" – at least not in the simple sense that this English word conveys. Instead, the Bible says that the sun, moon, and stars are to mark "religious festivals" or "sacred times." They are tokens or signs of God's covenants and His sovereign, benevolent care for His people. The Hebrew word behind this truth is *mo'edim* (moh-eh-DEEM). Usually, it is translated "festivals," but it means so much more – and this deeper revelation is vitally important to all that we're going to consider in this book. This word *mo'edim* means "a set or appointed time." It also means "appointed place, appointed meeting." It indicates to "signify" or "act as a sign."

Why is this important? This word reveals that God wants us to use the heavenly bodies to mark out divine encounters, appointed festivals and meetings with Him. It means that God has a sacred calendar, and He wants us to keep it. He wants us to use it as He has commanded in Scripture so that we experience His presence, receive His truth, and serve His purposes. This is one of the great biblical secrets. There is revelation in keeping the calendar of God.

God's calendar is so pregnant with meaning that one wise rabbi, the famous Rabbi Hirsch, said many years ago, "A Jew's catechism is his calendar." In other words, God has so coded truth into His set times, His seasons, and His festivals that those who understand them receive their truths and are irreversibly changed by them. The calendar becomes a catechism, as the good rabbi said. What's more, this isn't just true for Jews. It is true for all of us who serve the living God.

12

Now, to begin to understand God's sacred calendar, one must realize that God's calendar is based on a lunar (moon) cycle, not on a solar (sun) cycle. Most of us have lived our whole lives according to a solar calendar that is 365 days long. It is made up of twelve months of around thirty days, with many of those months named for ancient gods – like January after the god Janus (Roman god of beginnings) or February named for the god Februa (Roman festival of ritual purification) or March named for Mars, the ancient god of war. This solar year begins on January 1, ends on December 31, and has four seasons. This is likely the calendar you've used your whole life.

God's calendar is quite different. It's a lunar calendar. Psalm 104:19 tells us, "He appointed the moon for seasons." This truth underlies the whole of God's sacred calendar. It is His will, it is His way, and knowing this is the beginning of numbering our days aright. Yet there are also practical reasons for using a lunar calendar. The moon is far better for building a calendar upon than is the sun because the moon changes every night. It marks the progress of time much more efficiently. Also, nature seems to harmonize with the moon. From my time in the woods and forests, fields, lakes, and rivers, I have discovered that animals actually change their feeding times every day based on the cycle of the moon.

God appointed the moon for seasons.

It is His will.
It is His way.

This makes the lunar calendar more helpful for agriculture also, for example, because even the simplest farmer in the most rural setting can tell the stages of the moon just by looking in the night sky. Farmers have been governing their planting and harvesting by such lunar cycles for centuries and all while using only the naked eye.

The same could never be done using only the sun because the sun looks very much the same day to day. Let me put this in more modern terms. God has an iPhone. It's diamond encrusted by stars without number. It has one large stone right in the center, which is the moon. The calendar that you use on your iPhone has nothing to do with God's calendar. The beginning of God's year is not January 1, the birthday of His Son is not December 25, and resurrection day is not Easter. No, God's calendar is lunar. He defines times and seasons in entirely different terms. What you have on your cell phone or in your date book is commonly referred to as the Gregorian calendar. It is sometimes described as the Babylonian calendar.

If you'll begin calling the calendar you use the Babylonian calendar, it will help you remember that this calendar is far removed from the one that God originally intended. The first great truth of God's calendar is that it is a lunar calendar. The second marvelous revelation is that God's calendar uses months that are much different from those to which we have become accustomed.

We discover this by reading our Bibles. Time and again in the pages of Scripture, God date stamps events by using the names of months from His calendar that are foreign to those of us who are only used to the solar or Gregorian calendar. I'll list just a few verses of the Bible in which God times events using the months of His calendar:

> "The foundation of the temple of the LORD was laid in the fourth year, in the month of **Ziv** [zeev]" (1 Kings 6:37, NIV).

> "In the eleventh year in the month of **Bul** [bool], the eighth month, the temple was finished in all its details according to its specifications" (1 Kings 6:38, NIV).

> "All the Israelites came together to King Solomon at the time of the festival in the month of **Ethanim** [eth-ah-NEEM], the seventh month" (1 Kings 8:2, NIV).

> "The temple was completed on the third day of the month **Adar** [uh-DAHR], in the sixth year of the reign of King Darius" (Ezra 6:15, NIV).

> "The words of Nehemiah son of Hakaliah: 'In the month of **Kislev** [KEES-lev] in the twentieth year, while I was in the citadel of Susa. . . .'" (Nehemiah 1:1, NIV).

> "In the month of **Nisan** [NEE-sahn] in the twentieth year of King Artaxerxes, when wine was brought for him, I took the wine and gave it to the king" (Nehemiah 2:1, NIV).

Obviously, God assumes we will learn His calendar so we can understand the times and seasons He defines in the pages of the Bible for divine encounters. Yet knowing God's calendar is also important because when God does not date events by using the name of a month, He uses its number. This is an obvious call to know the order of the months in God's lunar calendar. Here are a few examples:

> "On the fifteenth day of the seventh month the LORD's Festival of Tabernacles begins, and it lasts for seven days" (Leviticus 23:34, NIV).

> "The LORD spoke to Moses in the tent of meeting in the Desert of Sinai on the first day of the second month of the second year after the Israelites came out of Egypt" (Numbers 1:1, NIV).

> "They are to do it on the fourteenth day of the second month at twilight" (Numbers 9:11, NIV).

> "On the fourteenth day of the first month the LORD's Passover is to be held" (Numbers 28:16, NIV).

> "On the tenth day of this seventh month hold a sacred assembly" (Numbers 29:7, NIV).

The months of the Hebrew calendar, then, are important for understanding God's set times for us to encounter His holy presence and discover and rediscover His plan and purpose for us. I'm going to list these months here, along with their approximate times in the Gregorian or solar calendar. This is also one of the great truths of God's calendar:

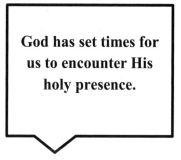

God has set times for us to encounter His holy presence.

the beginning, end, and seasons of God's year do not correspond to the beginning, end, and seasons of the solar year. There is a reason for this, as we will soon see. For now, though, let's take a look at the months of God in order and in their approximate setting in the solar calendar you use now.

	Name of Month	Occurrence in Solar Calendar
1.	Nisan (NEE-sahn)	March-April
2.	Iyar (EE-yahr) [called Ziv (zeev) in 1 Kings 6:1,37]	April-May
3.	Sivan (see-VAHN)	May-June
4.	Tammuz (tam-MOOZ)	June-July
5.	Av (ahv)	July-August
6.	Elul (el-OOL)	August-September
7.	Tishrei (tish-RAY) [Called Ethanim (ETH-uh-neem) in 1 Kings 8:2]	September-October
8.	Cheshvan (KESH-vahn) [Called Bul (bool) in 1 Kings 6:38]	October-November
9.	Kislev (KEES-lev)	November-December
10.	Tevet (teh-VEHT)	December-January
11.	Shevat (shuh-VAHT)	January-February
12.	Adar I (uh-DAHR)	February-March
12b.	Adar Beit[2] (uh-DAHR bait)	Leap Years

I'm throwing so many new ideas and terms at you that you might feel as though you have landed in a foreign country. You have! You have landed in the foreign country of God's celebrations, cycles, set times, and seasons. It may feel a bit foreign, but this is actually your native country. This is where you belong if you have surrendered your life to the living God by accepting Jesus Christ as Messiah, Lord, and Savior. It is only slightly foreign to you now because our churches have forgotten it, and we've lost the revelation of it. It's yours, though, and it is where you are called to dwell. Great things

---

[2] In a leap year, there are two months of Adar, the last month of the year. When that occurs, Adar I is thirty days long, and Adar II (Beit) is twenty-nine days long. A short Jewish year, therefore, consists of 353 to 355 days, while a leap year varies between 383 and 385 days. The reason for this is explained later in the book.

are about to be released into your life as you walk in this fresh revelation from and of God Almighty. Thus far, then, we have been positioned by three truths:

1. God's calendar is a lunar calendar, not the solar calendar with which we are accustomed.
2. God's calendar is comprised of months different from those in the calendar we use.
3. God's year is different from the year with which we are familiar.

There is a fourth profound truth we're about to realize. It is this: God's calendar is defined by His appointed feasts and His declared, sacred seasons that He has called us to celebrate. Put another way, God's calendar is for the sake of worship and divine encounters where He reveals His nature and character to us. It is a calendar that prompts us, much like a sacred alarm clock to arise and remember God's great deeds, to celebrate God's abundant goodness, and to worship God for His glorious acts yet to come.

This truth is not only a truth about calendars; it also the key to understanding the whole of the Bible, particularly the meaning of the life of Jesus Christ on earth. The fact that God's calendar is dotted with festivals and holy days is a revelation in itself. Yet when we understand the earthly life of Jesus in light of these festivals, the truth of who He is explodes into our lives. Here is a brief example of how understanding the feasts helps us understand the life of the Lord Jesus. Below are just a few Bible references to the Feast of Passover, yet when you read them you will discover how essential these verses are to understanding who Jesus is and what His sacrifice on the cruel, biting beam of Calvary really means to us.

> "As you know, the Passover is two days away – and the Son of Man [Jesus] will be handed over to be crucified" (Matthew 26:2, NIV).

> "Now the Passover and the Festival of Unleavened Bread were only two days away, and the chief priests and the teachers of the law were scheming to arrest Jesus secretly and kill him" (Mark 14:1, NIV).

"He said to them, 'I have eagerly desired to eat this Passover with you before I suffer'" (Luke 22:15, NIV).

"When it was almost time for the Jewish Passover, many went up from the country to Jerusalem for their ceremonial cleansing before the Passover" (John 11:55, NIV).

"Get rid of the old yeast, so that you may be a new unleavened batch – as you really are. For Christ, our Passover lamb, has been sacrificed" (1 Corinthians 5:7, NIV).

"Let us keep the Festival [feast], not with the old bread leavened with malice and wickedness, but with the unleavened bread of sincerity and truth" (1 Corinthians 5:8, NIV).

We can't fully understand the life of Jesus Christ on earth or what the Apostle Paul was teaching about the Lord Jesus if we don't understand the power of the Passover. So this feast becomes a key to the full revelation of the sacrifice of our Savior, the Passover Lamb of God. How thrilling this is, and how much revelation there is waiting for us in the calendar of God!

Let me employ another example. According to Acts 2, the Holy Spirit fell on 120 people in a house in Jerusalem on the Day of Pentecost. Yet where did the word *Pentecost* come from? What is its meaning? Why do we even speak of a Day of Pentecost? Well, Pentecost was also one of God's set times, a feast of harvest, a day set aside by God to acknowledge the magnificent yield He had provided for the people by His mighty hand. It also had a symbolic theme of the ingathering of the Gentile world. It makes perfect sense, then, that God poured out the Holy Spirit upon the early church on this particular declared and decreed feast day. Pentecost was a celebration of ingathering. The Holy Spirit was poured out upon believers, equipping and empowering them to be witnesses. They would have power to go and gather the human harvest of God from the far-flung corners of the earth. There was no other day with more prophetic significance for such an outpouring than the day of the Feast of Ingathering which had been decreed hundreds of years earlier by God Almighty –Pentecost!

Before I go more deeply into the matters I've introduced to you, allow me to address a possible misunderstanding. Am I trying to drag us back under the law by urging that we know and celebrate the sacred seasons of God? Absolutely, positively, unequivocally not! I simply desire for us to obey God and to see Him in the greater revelation that is available through His *mo'edim* – His signs and festivals. My goal here is not legalism. My goal is revelation and celebration. My deeper ambition is intimacy with God. You remember that I said understanding God's times and seasons is like a husband gaining insight into a wife so he can love, care for, and protect her in a greater way. This is exactly what God desires: that we draw closer to Him and walk in His ways. This is God's primary ambition. Even in something like the Jewish kosher laws – laws that define what is appropriate for Jews to eat and when – there is an invitation to intimacy with Almighty God.

Some would look at kosher laws and see only "do not taste, do not touch" – the arcane requirements and regulations of a restrictive God to force obedience with judgment and condemnation. Yet the deeper truth of kosher laws may well be that in the smallest and most mundane matters of life – something as simple as eating – we welcome God and acknowledge Him as the sustainer of life. Certainly, there is a physical benefit of kosher laws, but they are also a call to pause, reflect, and acknowledge God. In kosher requirements, the Jewish people are illustrating that we are not animals to eat what we please, when we please, and how we please. Through these laws, Jewish children learn patience, order, obedience, thankfulness, discipline, manners, and a revelation of God as provider and sustainer of their sustenance. We have a choice: focus only on the rules and the requirements, or look deeper and perceive the "language" of God through the law and the revelation of the One who gave the requirements.

Again, I am certainly not attempting in any way to place us back under the law and insist that all of us eat kosher. Not at all. I *am* determined by God's grace to help us recover the New Covenant purpose of much of God's Old Covenant requirements. That's what those of us who are in Christ are meant to do. As one of the early Church fathers said, "In the Old Testament the New Testament is concealed; in the New Testament the Old Testament is revealed." My heart's prayer is for us to receive the fullest revelation of God our Father through Jesus Christ by the power of the Holy Spirit.

WISDOM OF THE RABBIS

In each generation every individual is obliged to feel as though he or she personally came out of Egypt. . . . Therefore we are obliged to thank, praise, laud, glorify, and exalt, to honor, bless, extol, and adore Him who performed all these wonders for our ancestors and for us: He brought us out of slavery into freedom, out of sorrow into joy, out of mourning into a holiday, out of darkness into daylight, and out of bondage into redemption. Let us then sing before Him a new song: Halleluiah!
~The Passover Haggadah

On Rosh Hashanah all human beings pass before Him as troops, as it is said, "the Lord looks down from heaven, He sees all mankind. From His dwelling place He gazes on all the inhabitants of the earth, He who fashions the hearts of them all, who discerns all their doings." ~ Rabbi Dr. Reuven Hammer

On Yom Kippur [yohm kee-POOR], the ritual trial reaches its conclusion. The people finally drop all their defenses and excuses and throw themselves on the mercy of the court, yet the same people never lose the conviction that they will be pardoned. This atonement is by divine grace; it is above and beyond the individual effort or merit. ~ Rabbi Irving Greenberg

Yom Kippur is the idea that we get a second chance before God forgives us for the mistakes that we've made. And we all get a second chance in life. ~ Rabbi Shmuel Herzfeld

Chapter III

THE PATTERN OF GOD'S FEASTS: AN OVERVIEW

L et me give you a brief overview of the feasts of God; a "fly-over" if you will, so that you can begin to get the pattern of God's festivals clearly embedded in your heart. We will have to begin at the beginning, which in the Hebrew calendar is not January in winter but much more appropriately in the month of Nisan (NEE-sahn). And I'm not talking about the automobile! I remind you of the wise words of Rabbi Hirsch: "A Jew's catechism is his calendar." This is certainly true of the month of Nisan, the first month in the Hebrew calendar. The word *Nisan* is probably derived from two Hebrew words: *nitzan* (bud) and *nissim* (miracle). Perfect, isn't it?

The month Nisan occurs in spring (March-April), a time of new life and rebirth. It is this month in which God Almighty performed the miracle of delivering Israel out of Egyptian bondage and slavery, the singular event that quite literally gave birth to the nation of Israel. Do you see how ingeniously symbolic and prophetically accurate the Hebrew calendar is? There are two festival seasons within the Hebrew calendar: Spring Feasts and Fall Feasts. All of them are part of the powerful drama that began the Jewish nation.

THE SPRING FEASTS – SUPERNATURAL PEACE

Passover

According to God's command, Passover always begins on the fourteenth of Nisan. In Leviticus 23:5, the Lord told Moses, "The LORD's Passover begins at twilight on the fourteenth day of the first month" (NIV). On this night, all the people of Israel reenact the first Passover, which occurred in Egypt when God delivered His people from their 430 years of Egyptian bondage.

After all the plagues that had come upon Egypt, Pharaoh's heart was still hard, and he would not let the Hebrews go to worship their God. The final plague pronounced the death of the firstborn of every Egyptian. The Israelites were told that if they put the blood of their sacrificial lambs on their doorposts, the angel of death would "pass over their homes." This is how Passover got its name. (See Exodus 12:3-14.) Since that amazing day, the people of God have celebrated Passover and called to remembrance their glorious deliverance. The Lord God told Moses that the people were to eat lamb with bitter herbs and unleavened bread. They were to eat it all in haste with their shoes on, their robes tucked in their belts, and their staffs in their hands. In other words, they were to remember the urgency of that first night and be prepared to leave at once. Passover is a pilgrimage feast of Israel, which means it is one of the three feasts that God commanded all male Israelites to celebrate each year in Jerusalem.

> Since that amazing day, the people of God have celebrated Passover and called to remembrance their glorious deliverance.

The Feast of Unleavened Bread

The second Spring Feast of Israel is the Feast of Unleavened Bread. This feast commemorates the event that began the very next day after the first Passover in Egypt. At the same time God Almighty told His people to slaughter a lamb and to place its blood upon their doorposts so the curse of death would pass over them, He declared and decreed, "For seven days you are to eat bread made without yeast. On the first day remove the yeast from your houses, for whoever eats anything with yeast in it from the first day through the seventh must be cut off from Israel" (Exodus 12:15, NIV).

God called this the Feast of Unleavened Bread, and He said that it was important because it was "on this very day that I brought your divisions out of Egypt" (Exodus 12:17, NIV). Each year – in spring, on the fifteenth of Nisan, the day following Passover – the people removed all yeast from their houses, for yeast is symbolic of sin, and they ate only unleavened bread because that's what their ancestors had done when God delivered them from Egypt. This feast, which lasted a week, was a time of thrilling deliverance. We'll get into the details of this feast later, but it is exciting already to see that holiness and deliverance are linked together in this second of the seven feasts of Israel.

Firstfruits

The third Spring Feast of Israel was the Feast of Firstfruits, and it was a celebration of the goodness of the land that God gave to His people after their wilderness wanderings. This feast took place, surprisingly, on the first day of the week, a Sunday – the day after the Sabbath that occurred during the Feast of Unleavened Bread. In Leviticus 23:10-11, God decreed,

> "Speak to the children of Israel, and say to them: 'When you come into the land which I give to you, and reap its harvest, then you shall bring a sheaf of the firstfruits of your harvest to the priest. He shall wave the sheaf before the LORD, to be accepted on your behalf; on the day after the Sabbath the priest shall wave it'" (NKJV).

This feast may appear on the surface to be less important than the others of spring, but let me assure you that for the New Testament believer, the Feast of Firstfruits is one of the most significant and critical of all.

Pentecost – Supernatural Power

The fourth Spring Feast derives its name from the fact that it comes exactly fifty days after Firstfruits. As a result, it is referred to as the Feast of Weeks or *Shavuot* (sha-voo-OHT), the Hebrew word for "weeks." It is the second of the pilgrimage feasts of Israel. Here is how God commanded His people to observe this feast:

> "From the day after the Sabbath, the day you brought the sheaf of the wave offering, count off seven full weeks. Count off fifty days up to the day after the seventh Sabbath, and then present an offering of new grain to the LORD.

"From wherever you live, bring two loaves made of two-tenths of an ephah [EE-fah] of the finest flour, baked with yeast, as a wave offering of firstfruits to the LORD.

"Present with this bread seven male lambs, each a year old and without defect, one young bull and two rams. They will be a burnt offering to the LORD, together with their grain offerings and drink offerings – a food offering, an aroma pleasing to the LORD.

"Then sacrifice one male goat for a sin offering and two lambs, each a year old, for a fellowship offering. The priest is to wave the two lambs before the LORD as a wave offering, together with the bread of the firstfruits. They are a sacred offering to the LORD for the priest. On that same day you are to proclaim a sacred assembly and do no regular work. This is to be a lasting ordinance for the generations to come, wherever you live" (Leviticus 23:15-21, NIV).

This was a harvest feast, a set time to celebrate the greater yield of the later harvest that came fifty days after the early harvest of Firstfruits. Yet it also contains elements that seem to signify a greater reach than was represented in the pure celebrations of Passover, the Feast of Unleavened Bread, and Firstfruits. Only leavened bread is used in this Feast of Weeks. This may signify that God had the Gentile world in mind, which was represented by "unclean" leaven. That would be perfectly in keeping with what took place on this day centuries later.

You see, the Greek name for this feast is *Pentecost*, which also means "fifty." When the Holy Spirit was poured out upon the early church on the Day of Pentecost, many nations were immediately impacted. Perhaps in this Feast of Weeks, God was teaching His people that they were meant to reach the world and that one day He would pour out the Holy Spirit upon His people to empower and propel them to do just that: go to all nations.

These Spring Feasts of God – Passover, the Feast of Unleavened Bread, the Feast of Firstfruits, and the Feast of Weeks (or Pentecost) – are divinely declared celebrations to commemorate the great deliverance from bondage in Egypt, purity among God's people, the richness of the Promised Land, and the calling of God's people to reach the nations of the earth.

THE FALL FEASTS – SUPERNATURAL PRESENCE

The Fall Feasts of God began many months after the Feast of Weeks or Pentecost in the seventh month of the Hebrew calendar, Tishrei. The closeness of Passover and Pentecost and the fact that a great deal of time separates them from the Fall Feasts are very symbolic and prophetic, as we will discover. That these later feasts began in the seventh month gives us some indication about their theme and message. They celebrate completion, with judgment and with new beginnings.

The Feast of Trumpets

The first fall festival of God began, as we might expect, on the first day of the seventh month. On the first of Tishrei, there was to be a great assembly, the major feature of which was the blowing of trumpets. The Lord had told Moses,

> "Speak unto the children of Israel, saying, In the seventh month, in the first day of the month, shall ye have a sabbath, a memorial of blowing of trumpets, an holy convocation" (Leviticus 23:24).

The trumpet or *shofar* (show-FAHR) is often our Father's instrument of choice. It was used for many purposes, but at the beginning of the Fall Feasts, we learn that it was employed for both a wake-up call for the people of God and a summons to repentance.

This urgent call to consecration was necessary because the Feast of Trumpets came ten days before the holiest day of the Hebrew year, the Day of Atonement. During these ten days, the people of Israel were to repent of their sins and make right any wrongs they could before they reached the Day of Atonement or Yom Kippur, a day of judgment for God's people.

The Day of Atonement – Yom Kippur

The most significant high holy day of the entire Jewish year was the Day of Atonement. God Almighty spoke the decree directly to Moses:

"The tenth day of this seventh month shall be the Day of Atonement. It shall be a holy convocation for you; you shall afflict your souls, and offer an offering made by fire to the LORD" (Leviticus 23:27, NKJV).

This daunting, weighty, and fearsome day was for the deepest introspection and self-examination. It was the day upon which the people of Israel were most aware of their personal and national sins, and the high priest entered the Holy of Holies, the singular place of the most tangible presence of the Almighty on planet Earth. The high priest was commanded and permitted to enter the Holy of Holies only on this one day of the year. The people were forbidden to do any work. It was the most solemn of occasions. Wrongs were grieved. Destinies were decided. Judgments were handed down. God, the Lord on High, judged all things on the Day of Atonement.

The Feast of Tabernacles

The seventh and concluding celebration of the year was the Feast of Tabernacles, the third of the Fall Feasts of God and the third of the pilgrimage feasts. Trumpets had come on the first day of Tishrei, the Day of Atonement or Yom Kippur came on the tenth day, and finally the Feast of Tabernacles commenced on the fifteenth day of the seventh month. It was a set time that continued for seven days. That this was the seventh feast, that it took place in the seventh month, and that it lasted seven days are prophetic and all the evidence we need to be sure that this feast was of the highest priority to the living God. Its purpose was to remember how, by supernatural and miraculous means, the Lord, Jehovah Jireh, had provided for the Israelites in the wilderness. Here is the divine decree:

"You shall dwell in booths for seven days. All who are native Israelites shall dwell in booths, that your generations may know that I made the children of Israel dwell in booths when I brought them out of the land of Egypt: I am the Lord your God" (Leviticus 23:42-43, NKJV).

The instruction was implicit – the Israelites were to live in booths each year to remember His provision for them as they wandered through the treacherous wilderness before entering the Promised Land. Yet there seems to be another, more universal purpose of this seventh and final feast. It is the single feast that is mentioned in

Scripture as eventually being required of all nations if they are to come under the blessing of God. God will one day require that all nations of this planet acknow-ledge His provision – yes, to Israel in the wilderness centuries ago, but more broadly the provision of God for all men in a multitude of ways. We will examine the symbolism of the Feast of Tabernacles more fully in the pages to come, but for now it is important to realize that the seventh feast of God, taking place in the seventh month and being eventually required for all nations, is a direct indication of the prophetic power and profound importance of this set time of celebration.

So we see that there are seven feasts of God.

Four commence in spring:

- The Day of Passover
- The weeklong Feast of Unleavened Bread
- Feast of Firstfruits
- The Feast of Weeks

In the fall there are three feasts:

- The Feast of Trumpets
- The Day of Atonement
- The Feast of Tabernacles

These are the Big Seven – the major feasts of God as commanded and described in the Bible, decreed by our Father God. I should mention briefly in our discussion of this glorious subject that Jewish people today celebrate two other feasts that are not commanded in Scripture. One is Hanukkah, a celebration of the rededication of the Temple by the Maccabees around 165 BC, and the other is Purim (poo-REEM), a celebration of the events described in the book of Esther. Both are important and I'll describe the powerful symbolism of Purim later, but we must be careful not to confuse them with God's original seven feasts in Scripture. Much of what we've covered in this brief flyover of the feasts may be new to you. This is a revelation-rich portion of the heritage of all of God's people. We are studying His divine calendar and God's truth symbolized and revealed in these feasts. Let us master these patterns and embrace God's truth. These are the *mo'edim*, the sacred signs, of God for all of His people.

27

❦ ❦ ❦

WISDOM OF THE RABBIS

I believe we are living in the time of Elul and God is calling us to repentance. The trumpet is about to sound, signifying our Messiah's return. Those who are living for Him long for this day and will see it as a wonderful time of joy and triumph. But those who are not right with God will experience dread and destruction. ~ *Rabbi Jonathan Bernis*

When Jews appear for Divine judgment, the angels say to them: "Don't be afraid, the Judge . . . is your Father."
~ *Midrash Tehillim*

❧ ❧ ❧

Chapter IV

THE RED BLOOD MOONS

Allow me to implore you to complete a special task before starting this chapter – a homework assignment if you will. Whether your home is on the banks of the Jordan River or deep in the hills of eastern Kentucky, I ask you to take a moment to observe the grand and glorious fourth day of creation. "Fourth day of creation?" you ask. That's right, friends. I want you to walk outdoors, look up at the vast expanse above, and thank our heavenly Father for creating light by day and by night.

After all, when was the last time you watched the sun set and the moon rise? If you would only carve out a mere few minutes to watch the dusty red horizon cloak itself in a cover of moonlit darkness, you could see the heavens open up like a rose in spring bloom, unfolding illuminations as each star is slowly revealed. It's quite marvelous, isn't it? Whenever I have the opportunity to stop and drink in these celestial lights, I become overwhelmed by the magnitude of God. I feel just as David expressed in Psalm 19:1-4:

"The heavens declare the glory of God,
    and the sky displays what his hands have made. . . .
Their sound has gone out into the entire world,
    their message to the ends of the earth" (GW).

When I take in the glory of our Creator's handiwork in the endless night sky, I am amazed that what I am witnessing was set in motion by God before the foundations of the earth were set. Before your mother ever saw the twinkle in your father's eye, God was speaking the twinkle of cosmic entities into existence. Scientists say that the light you view in the night cosmos was actually emitted hundreds of years ago. Science reveals that what you observe above in the evening has been traveling for light-years to arrive at a point where the naked eye can see it. It is not as though some being in the heavens turned on a lamp the moment you began looking upward! Those lights have been in transit at times for centuries.

But it is not the science of the sky that fascinates me. Rather, the Creator of the universe and His heavenly splendor fill me with awe-struck wonder. An overwhelming thought is that on the fourth day of creation, our Father formed the sun to bring us light and warmth by day and the moon to illuminate the night. Of course, my words cannot compare to what the Bible declares regarding this fourth-day miracle. Genesis 1:14-18 describes it beautifully:

> "God said, Let there be lights in the firmament of the heaven to divide the day from the night; and let them be for signs, and for seasons, and for days, and years: And let them be for lights in the firmament of the heaven to give light upon the earth: and it was so.

> "And God made two great lights; the greater light to rule the day, and the lesser light to rule the night: he made the stars also. And God set them in the firmament of the heaven to give light upon the earth, and to rule over the day and over the night, and to divide the light from the darkness: and God saw that it was good."

So the sky that glowed so gloriously on the evening you were married or the night your child was born – everything that caused that sky to exist on those important days – was set in motion on the fourth day of creation. Our all-knowing, all-powerful God put His divine machinery in motion so that the sky above you would appear in the exact arrangement you saw on that day.

I want you to know this because it is foundational to what I'm going to unveil regarding the phenomenon of Red Blood Moons. If you don't keep this truth in mind about all that God set in motion on the fourth day of creation, you could become caught up, even swept away, in the apocalyptic rhetoric surrounding Red Blood Moons that is sweeping through our culture.

If you remember that everything you behold in the sky at any given moment was planned and set in motion by God on the fourth day of creation, then your attention will be not on the latest end-time theories or predictions but on the real question: Why would God program His celestial bodies to bring these signs into view now? This is the real issue!

★

A naturally occurring galactic phenomenon is known as a Red Blood Moon (or some say Blood Red Moon). I have heard critics say that some overexcited preachers gave this phenomenon its dramatic name just to get people stirred up. Not true! NASA borrowed the ancient name for a "Hunter's Moon" or "Red Blood Moon" and so made it the official modern term.[3] Trust me, NASA employees are about the most even-tempered, emotionally steady people you'd ever want to meet! They certainly did not start using this name for dramatic reasons. In my opinion, the name is appropriate because they were describing a moon that is blood red in color. Thus, Red Blood Moon. Mystery solved!

The moon shows brightly in our night sky because it reflects the light of the sun. The moon has no light of its own; it only reflects a source of light that comes from beyond itself. Several interesting descriptions of the church appear in Song of Solomon 6:10. One of them is that she is "fair as the moon." How appropriate that we, as the church, have no shine, light, power, or glory of our own but are called and equipped to reflect those characteristics of our Father, but that's for another book! This has been the theme of volumes of poetry, songs, and sermons, but we won't take time for such romantic considerations now.

She is fair as the moon.

Occasionally, the sun, moon, and earth align in such a way that the earth blocks the light from the sun that would normally shine on the moon. When this happens, the moon appears darkened and eerie in the night sky. This is called a lunar eclipse. Perhaps you've seen this from time to time through the years, or you've seen some of the dramatic photographs of this phenomenon. When the earth completely blocks the light from the sun, the moon tends to appear reddish in color. This is a result of the way the sun's light passes through earth's atmosphere and bends toward the moon. Strangely, our

---

[3] http://www.nasa.gov/vision/universe/watchtheskies/13oct_lunareclipse.html.

planet's atmosphere filters the light of the sun and blocks most of the colors in the spectrum. But during this marvelous wonder, red light is permitted to pass through and splashes upon the moon. This creates the vivid and memorable sight of a Red Blood Moon. These Red Blood Moons have happened from time to time throughout history and continue today. They are somewhat rare, and we probably wouldn't be paying so much attention to them today if their only oddity were this matter of color.

What has brought Red Blood Moons to our headlines today is that at times – though very, very rarely – this phenomenon occurs in a series of four. The sophisticated word for this is *tetrad*. It means four in a row during a defined period of time. So you can imagine that if a Red Blood Moon is rare, having four of them in a row almost never happens.

Now let's add another layer of rarity. Suppose we look only at the Red Blood Moons that have occurred in history and that also coincide with some of the Jewish feasts we surveyed in the last chapter. Suppose we remember that God placed the sun, moon, and stars in the heavens to delineate sacred seasons and ceremonies, and suppose we ask ourselves if these Red Blood Moon tetrads ever coincided with the Hebrew calendar and Jewish feasts in a way that signals their significance.

Remember that the Hebrew word *mo'edim,* the word often translated "feasts" or "festivals," actually means "signs" or "symbols." So our question becomes, Are these tetrads of Red Blood Moons signifying anything to us?

I think you'll see that they are.

First, in Jewish tradition the occurrence of Red Blood Moons has most often been taken as a sign of war. The Jewish people have historically considered them bad omens, usually relating to bloodshed. The Jewish Talmud (TAL-mood), the commentary of the ancient rabbis upon the Torah, declares, "When the moon is in eclipse, it is a bad omen for Israel. If its face is as red as blood, the sword is coming to the world." Armed with this knowledge, let's survey some of the times in history when a tetrad of Red Blood Moons coincided with important dates on the Hebrew calendar that signaled historic events on earth.

1. The Crucifixion of Jesus

A Red Blood Moon tetrad occurred during AD 32 and 33, the period when our Lord Jesus Christ was crucified on the angry, mean, biting beam of Calvary. These blood moons coincided with Passover and the Feast of Tabernacles in these years.[4]

2. Jewish Persecution

Four total lunar eclipses occurred on Passover and the Feast of Tabernacles in AD 161 and 163, coinciding with the worst persecution of the Jewish people up to that time.[5]

3. Defeat of the Arabs

Four total lunar eclipses occurred on Passover and on Yom Kippur in AD 795 and 796 when Charlemagne, emperor of the Holy Roman Empire, established a buffer between France and Spain, ending centuries of Arab incursion into Western Europe.[6]

4. Another Defeat of the Arabs

Four total lunar eclipses occurred in 842–843 when Muslims from Africa attacked and looted Rome. Shortly after these eclipses, in 860–861, the Byzantine Empire defeated Arab armies at a great battle in what is now Turkey and permanently stopped the Islamic infiltration of Eastern Europe.[7]

5. The Expulsion of the Jews from Spain

Four total lunar eclipses occurred in 1493–1494, only months after King Ferdinand and Queen Isabella of Spain expelled the Jews from that nation, commissioned Christopher Columbus to sail to the New World, and ended the Spanish Inquisition. We

---

[4] There is voluminous information regarding lunar eclipses at NASA.gov and specific data about their occurrence in history at http://eclipse.gsfc.nasa.gov/LEcat5/appearance.html.
[5] Ibid.
[6] Ibid.
[7] Ibid.

know the exact dates of these Red Blood Moons and how they coincided with the Hebrew calendar.[8]

6. The Jewish War of Independence

In 1948, the United Nations voted in favor of statehood for the nation of Israel, and she took her place among the nations of the world. Israel was immediately forced to defend her newly gained independence against the surrounding Arab nations, a conflict that continues to this day. In the years that immediately followed Israeli independence, Red Blood Moons occurred according to this pattern on the Hebrew calendar:[9]

- Passover, April 13, 1949
- Feast of Tabernacles, October 7, 1949
- Passover, April 2, 1950
- Feast of Tabernacles, September 26, 1950

7. The Six-Day War

Though this 1967 war was in one sense a continuation of the ongoing conflict between Israel and her Arab enemies, the war was particularly significant because a result of this series of battles was that Jerusalem was reunited with the Jewish people for the first time in nearly nineteen hundred years. The story of this war is so replete with miracles that it reads like a page from the Bible. However, equally miraculous is the fact that a tetrad of Red Blood Moons occurred at that time, and once again, they fell on Passover and the Feast of Tabernacles.[10] Specifically, they occurred on:

- Passover, April 24, 1967
- Feast of Tabernacles, October 18, 1967
- Passover, April 13, 1968
- Feast of Tabernacles, October 6, 1968

You can see a pattern forming. Not only do we have the rare reoccurrence of a tetrad of Red Blood Moons, but we also have the even more rare alignment of the Red Blood Moon phenomenon with

---

[8] Ibid.

[9] Ibid.

[10] Ibid.

Hebrew holy days. That this alignment also transpired on some of the most significant dates in Israel's history is too much to be a coincidence. What is the Lord of history telling us? What is the meaning of these *mo'edim*? What are we meant to understand?

Let us consider the celestial clues and mark them well. As I might say if I were preaching, "We're about to see a thing! Speak on, Holy Ghost!"

Remember that our God is a God of cycles and patterns, of times and seasons. We must become historians, taught by the Holy Spirit, who consider the meaning of God's time stamps. For example, look at what just one date on the Hebrew calendar, the ninth day of the month of Av, the fifth month of the Jewish year, has to show us.

On this single date some of the worst events in the history of the Jewish people occurred:[11]

- In 1313 BC, the children of Israel cried out to God and declared that they would rather go back to Egypt than enter the Promised Land (Numbers 14).

- In 423 BC, the Babylonians destroyed the Temple of God.

- In AD 70 the Temple of God was again destroyed, this time by Roman armies.

- In AD 133, the famous Simon Bar Kochba rebellion of the Jews against Roman rule occurred.

- In 1095, Pope Urban II launched the First Crusade to the Holy Land.

- In 1290, King Edward I expelled the Jewish people from England.

- In 1492, King Ferdinand and Queen Isabella expelled the Jews from Spain.

---

[11] http://www.chabad.org/library/article_cdo/aid/946703/jewish/What-happened-on-the-Ninth-of-Av.htm.

- In 1914, World War I began. Historians consider World War II – with its Jewish ghettoes and concentration camps – the continuation of this First World War.

Are you beginning to see how vitally important it is that we view time through the lens of God's calendar and His celestial clues? Do you see that when we use His calendar, consider His signs in the heavens, and understand the spiritual battles that are taking place on the earth, we begin to receive tremendous revelation of our great God?

For example, historians are often amazed that through the centuries the early fall months of any given year are frequently filled with fantastic conflicts and epic events. It seems that the earth and its inhabitants begin to convulse and contract, rock and reel under some kind of supernatural power. Well, I believe that's exactly what happens. Why should this be? Perhaps the devil knows that great destinies are in play during the Fall Feasts of Israel. Perhaps it is the result and indication of the invisible war for God's purposes on earth as it rages during these fall months because the feasts of Israel are designed and divinely directed to release overwhelming power to God's people at specific times on God's calendar.

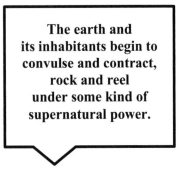

The earth and its inhabitants begin to convulse and contract, rock and reel under some kind of supernatural power.

These fall months are also the most financially troubled of all months. They are historically the worst months of the US Stock Exchange. The stock market collapse known as the Great Depression began during October 1929. October 19, 1987, is the famous Black Monday during which the market lost 22 percent of its value, the worst day of losses since the Great Depression. Don't forget that on September 17, 2001, just days after the disastrous events of September 11, 2001, the stock market lost 685 points in a single day. There is no question, fall is a troubled time. Consider this: James Foley, an American journalist, was kidnapped by the Islamic State and beheaded as Islamic extremists mocked. That happened in August

2014. Steven Sotloff, a Jew and an American journalist, was beheaded by the Islamic State in September 2014. David Haines, a forty-four-year-old British humanitarian and engineer, was also beheaded by the Islamic State in the fall on September 13, 2014.

I could give you pages of such data, and all of it would confirm that the fall months, during the Fall Feasts of Israel, are markedly the most troubled times of the year.

Now, let me present one of the main reasons this is all so important to us. We already know when the next tetrad of Red Blood Moons is going to occur. We are already into that tetrad as I write these words. Thanks to NASA computers, I can tell you the exact dates for this tetrad.[12] Carefully consider the following:

- First Day of Passover, April 15, 2014
- First Day of Sukkot, October 8, 2014
- First Day of Passover, April 4, 2015
- First Day of Sukkot, September 28, 2015

Now let me add yet another layer of alignment to our understanding of the Blood Red Moons in 2015. You probably already know that under the law of God and in the economy of Israel, every fifty years is a Jubilee year according to Leviticus 25:8-9:

"Thou shalt number seven sabbaths of years unto thee, seven times seven years; and the space of the seven sabbaths of years shall be unto thee forty and nine years. Then shalt thou cause the trumpet of the jubilee to sound on the tenth day of the seventh month, in the day of atonement shall ye make the trumpet sound throughout all your land."

All debts are forgiven, all slaves are freed, and the land is given rest. Every seventh year is also a Sabbath or sabbatical year, which in Hebrew is called a *Shemittah* (SHMIH-tah) year. In this year the people rest, and the land is allowed to lie fallow. God takes His Sabbaths – His weekly Sabbath, His seven-year Sabbath, and His fifty-year Sabbath – very seriously. They are "holy unto the Lord." In Jewish tradition, one who commits murder, idolatry, and sexual immorality is driven from the land – as is someone who violates the

---

[12] http://eclipse.gsfc.nasa.gov/lunar.html.

laws of Shemittah! More than once, God drove Israel from her land for violating the Sabbath. To understand this, you should know that in God's mind rest is an act of worship. It is not just ceasing from labor. It is pausing in the hurriedness of our lives and saying to God, *I do not have what I have through my own labors. You are my Provider. I can rest and still prosper since you are my God.*

So these Shemittah years have great significance. Shemittah began on September 25, 2014, and will end on September 13, 2015, the same year in which a tetrad of Red Blood Moons coincides with the feasts of God. Yes, 2015 concludes a Sabbath year, a Shemittah year, in which the people of God are meant to enter in a God-given rest.

So what are we to make of all this?

I want to be clear: I am not among those who claim doom and gloom on the basis of Red Blood Moons. I believe that an apocalyptic industry is operating in our world that draws a huge amount of attention by making outlandish claims at the slightest provocation. Doing this generates fear, confusion, and retreat from God's people rather than the victory that belongs to believers in Christ Jesus.

There are two lines of evidence that confirm that God does not want us to respond to the events going on around us with fear and trembling. The first of these is the clear testimony of the word of God, in passages such as these:

"God hath not appointed us to wrath" (1 Thessalonians 5:9).

"The path of the righteous is like the light of dawn, that shines brighter and brighter until the full day" (Proverbs 4:18 NASB).

"God hath not given us the spirit of fear; but of power, and of love, and of a sound mind" (2 Timothy 1:7).

"Perfect love casteth out fear" (1 John 4:18).

In addition, God gives us a choice about how we are going to react to the signs of the times. Historically, one of the greatest controversies in the church world has been the tension between the sovereignty of God and man's free moral agency. God gives us both the right and the ability to choose what we are going to believe. Here's what Moses told the children of Israel in Deuteronomy 30:19:

"I call heaven and earth to record this day against you, that I have set before you life and death, blessing and cursing: therefore choose life, that both thou and thy seed may live..."

Some people attribute everything that happens in their lives to the usually ill-defined concept of destiny. I am convinced that whether or not God's will is done either in an individual life or in a nation has much more to do with decisions than destiny. Here is another line of evidence to encourage you that we should be looking up instead of down, forward instead of backward, and anticipating blessing instead of cursing. According to the Jewish calendar, this year, which began at Rosh Hashanah (rahsh hah-SHAH-nah), is the year 5775, rather than 2015 on the Gregorian calendar. Keep in mind that all letters in the Hebrew alphabet have a numeric value assigned to them, as well as a pictorial symbol. The symbol for the Hebrew number 70, which is the decade in which we're living according to the Jewish calendar, is the letter ayin (aye-EEN). This is the approximate equivalent of the years 2010 to 2020 in the Gregorian calendar. (We might go so far as to say we're living in the 70s.)

> **God's will has much more to do with decisions than destiny.**

The pictorial form of ayin is a symbol with two heads, or eyes, on top. These indicate seeing, understanding and obeying the prophetic insight available to us. It is important to note there are two eyes, not just one. This is significant because two indicates a choice that must be made. We can either approach our future with fear or faith – with a positive expectation or a negative attitude. The choice is ours.

The direction of our lives and the outcomes we experience are, in most cases, a direct result of the way we choose to look at the circumstances around us.

Once there were twin boys who wanted a pony for Christmas. On Christmas morning, their parents took them to a barn and opened a stall door. The stall was packed with manure. The pessimist started complaining, "This is terrible! I never get what I want!" His brother, the optimist, grabbed a shovel and began digging.

The pessimist said, "What in the world are you doing?" This is nothing but a big mess!" His optimistic brother said, "With all this manure, there's got to be a pony in here somewhere!"

Be encouraged, my friend, God rules and reigns over all His creation, and He has your good in mind. You will find it as you look for it, whether in the everyday affairs of life or in the signs in the heavens.

Once again, the truth is that anything taking place in the heavens today was put in place and set in motion by God on the fourth day of creation. The Red Blood Moons of 2014 and 2015 are not last-minute announcements of judgment that caught God off guard and He responded to them, a few days after September 11, 2001. No, they are signs that God set in motion from the beginning of creation.

They are also not signals that God is angry with us. No, He loves us. He simply can't stop loving us! Romans 5:5-9 tells us:

"Hope maketh not ashamed; because the love of God is shed abroad in our hearts by the Holy Ghost which is given unto us. For when we were yet without strength, in due time Christ died for the ungodly. For scarcely for a righteous man will one die: yet peradventure for a good man some would even dare to die. But God commendeth his love toward us, in that, while we were yet sinners, Christ died for us. Much more then, being now justified by his blood, we shall be saved from wrath through him."

Our heavenly Father's purpose is to bless us. His desire is for us to draw near to Him, not for us to shrink away from Him in fear. Certainly His holiness compels Him to deal with the sin of the world; our sins are forgiven in Christ Jesus. God's wrath does not rest upon us. It rested on Jesus Christ as He was bolted upon that tree in our place. Oh, what glorious news that God's love rests upon us! I believe that His celestial signs in the skies and the unusual alignment of heavenly bodies and earthly dates that we are experiencing now are evidence of God's love and desire to bless His people in the midst of a tortured and troubled world.

We must never forget that while Red Blood Moons are aligning with God's feasts in 2015, that year is also a Shemittah year – a year of rest, provision, liberty, and peace for God's people. Could it be that God placed these signs in the heavens now to remind us of that very fact? Perhaps He wanted to remind us of the week of creation. Perhaps He wanted to remind us that He holds all things together by the power of His word (Hebrews 1:3). Perhaps He is saying, "I am here, and I have you in the palm of My hand. Fear not." Wouldn't it be just like our great God and loving Father to write of His love for us on the scroll of the heavens just to reassure us as we live in this tumultuous generation? I think so. I'm sure of it!

I'm also convinced that it would be scripturally accurate and make perfect sense for our Canaan King, Jesus Christ, to make His triumphant return to this planet during the feast season of Tabernacles, perhaps during the Feast of Trumpets, splitting the eastern skies and riding on that steaming white stallion (Revelation 19:11). That the next Feast of Trumpets after I write these words will be in a Shemittah year and during a tetrad of Red Blood Moons makes me wonder whether Jesus might seize the opportunity to make His second advent on the Feast of Trumpets 2015.

Wouldn't that be something? Let me tell you, though, I'm not about to make that prediction. Christians have embarrassed themselves too many times through the years by trying to predict when Jesus will return. I don't plan to join their number. I do, however, plan to be purified by the hope of His appearing, and you will find me saying quite often – on nearly every day of my life – "Even so, come quickly, Lord Jesus." But don't leave these pages thinking I've predicted the return of Christ. I haven't. I'm just eager for my Lord to return.

Here is my prediction, and I urge you to make it your prediction – and your confession – too: "Jesus is coming back – and until He does, I plan to walk in His blessing and serve Him with every fiber of my being."

"Even so: Come, Lord Jesus!"

Wisdom of the Rabbis

Pesach is not only about "freedom from." It is about our having the freedom to make the world a more sacred place by expanding God's presence in it.

~ Rabbi David A. Teutsch

This transformation from potential to actual required a supernatural jump provided by God. That's the essence of Pesach. We all want more meaning. We'd like to have a transcendent experience. But it's a struggle to work on spiritual growth. It's hard. It requires change. During Pesach we have the rare opportunity of using God's jumper cables. Take the opportunity that's there and ask God to give you the boost you've been waiting for.

~ Rabbi Max Weiman

Chapter V

THE FEASTS OF GOD: THE SPRING FESTIVALS

Passover

Sh'ma Yisra'el Adonai Eloheinu Adonai Echad.
V'ahavta et Adonai Elohecha,
b'chol l'vavcha uv'chol nafsh'cha uv'chol m'odecha.

Hear Israel, the Lord our God is one Lord.
And you shall love the Lord your God
with all your heart and with all your soul
and with all your strength.

My heart stirs each time I hear these words. They are the words of the great *Shema* (sheh-MAH) of Deuteronomy 6:4, perhaps the most cherished verse of the Torah through the centuries. The name for this verse comes from its first two words in the original Hebrew: "*Shema Yisrael*" or "Hear, O Israel." When Jesus was asked in Matthew 22:36, "Teacher, which is the greatest commandment in the law?" (NKJV). He answered by quoting the *Shema.* These words encapsulate all that God asks of those who serve Him. From the day of Adam to the last trumpet, this is the call of God upon the human heart.

This revered verse also stirs me because it inaugurates the Feast of Passover each year and has done so for generations. It is prayed each morning and each evening of the Passover celebration and all the sacred days that follow it. It calls men to know their God, to love Him unreservedly, and to offer before Him all of their gifts and their deepest hopes.

It is fitting that these words should be wrapped around the Great Feast, for Passover is the feast of God's redemption, a redemption that deserves to be answered just as the *Shema* describes: by hearing

God's word more carefully, by loving the Lord more fully, and by sacrificing before Him more completely.

You likely already know the story of Israel's first Passover, but come with me now as we touch again upon this historic moment – the moment in which a people born of the family of a single man was transformed into a nation that would forever change the world.

Scholars tell us that the great Exodus of Israel out of Egypt likely occurred in 1446 BC. During the more than four hundred years before that, Egypt had enslaved the Hebrews and made them objects of hatred and abuse. Though the wise Hebrew ruler Joseph had once saved all of Egypt and brought honor to the Jews, the good he had done was forgotten.

Our Bibles tell us that there arose in Egypt a Pharaoh who "knew not Joseph" (Exodus 1:8), who did not remember or honor the salvation won at Joseph's hand. A new Pharaoh and all those who came after him for 430 years treated the Jews as a people deserving only the shackle and the lash.

The Hebrews became an enslaved race – without heritage, without legacy, without possessions, without reward for their labors, and seemingly without any greater purpose in the world than to build the idolatrous monuments of Egypt. Then came Moses, who spoke God's fierce command to Pharaoh: "Let my people go!" But Pharaoh would not. So hard was his heart. So devoted was he to his false gods. In answer, the God of Moses sent plagues: water turned to blood, frogs, lice, flies, boils, hail, locusts, and darkness. All of it was visited upon Egypt while the Hebrews, in their divinely protected land of Goshen, were spared each time.

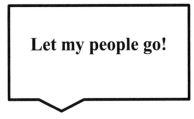

Let my people go!

Yet Pharaoh's heart grew harder. Finally, God determined to punish Egypt by slaying the firstborn of the land. We read in Exodus 12:2-8 the instructions he gave Moses in that desperate hour:

"This month is to be for you the first month, the first month of your year. Tell the whole community of Israel that on the tenth day of this month each man is to take a lamb for his family, one for each household. . . .

"Take care of them until the fourteenth day of the month, when all the members of the community of Israel must slaughter them at twilight. Then they are to take some of the blood and put it on the sides and tops of the doorframes of the houses where they eat the lambs" (NIV).

The Israelites did as commanded. God, in turn, kept His all-important promise: "When I see the blood, I will pass over you" (Exodus 12:13, NIV).

You know what unfolded thereafter. The firstborn of Egypt died that same night. Not a single family was left untouched by death. Grief filled the land. The next morning, the people of God were allowed – no, begged by the terrified Egyptians – to leave the land of their bondage.

The Israelites went, carrying with them the wealth the Egyptians heaped upon them. They miraculously passed through the Red Sea on dry land and then began the wilderness wanderings that would fashion them into a people prepared to occupy a land of their own.

It would take time – far too much time, it turned out, due to their rebellion and idolatry – but the day would come when they would enter the Promised Land.

Thus was a nation born out of bondage.

You know this history, but I retell it to draw from the tale of the first Passover the pattern of God for Passovers of all time. Clearly, God was fashioning more than a one-time deliverance in 1446 BC. Even while He instructed Moses about what should be done at that critical moment in Egypt, He already had His eye upon all Passovers throughout history.

It is why, before He spoke of lambs and blood on doorposts, He first said, "This month is to be for you the first month, the first month of your year. Tell the whole community of Israel that on the tenth day of this month . . ." (Exodus 12:2-3, NIV).

The month of Nisan starts the Hebrew calendar just as the event that first happened in it started the Hebrew people as a nation. It would be on the tenth of this month that the Hebrew people would choose their lambs. It would be on the fourteenth of this month that these lambs would be sacrificed and the blood placed upon the doorposts of the houses of the Hebrews. This month and these dates would be remembered forever and relived in Passover observances to come for generations.

There is meaning in each detail. Notice, for example, that each Hebrew family would choose its lamb and live with it for four days before sacrificing it to God. The Hebrews were shepherds. They were close to their flocks. They would know their sacrificial lamb intimately. In fact, they were commanded to know it.

They were commanded to be sure that the sacrifice had no blemishes. Yet that made them a stench in the nostrils of the Egyptians. Our Bibles tell us that the very reason that the Hebrews lived in the region of Egypt called Goshen, removed from the Egyptian people, was that "all shepherds are detestable to the Egyptians" (Genesis 46:34, NIV).

What I want you to see, though, is that from the moment God first gave instructions about the Passover in Egypt, He was already giving instructions about the pattern of the Passover feast. It is fascinating to observe. Calamity is about to befall Egypt. The people of Israel are shortly to pull up stakes and leave the land where they endured centuries of slavery.

Everything is changing and changing quickly. Yet God, who is never in a hurry, calmly gives Moses instructions for the Passover observances that will define generations yet to come:

> "Obey these instructions as a lasting ordinance for you and your descendants. When you enter the land that the LORD will give you as he promised, observe this ceremony. And when your children ask you, 'What does this ceremony mean to you?' then tell them, 'It is the Passover sacrifice to the LORD, who passed over the houses of the Israelites in Egypt and spared our homes when he struck down the Egyptians'" (Exodus 12:24-27, NIV).

Our God, who thinks in times and seasons and cycles, was from the very beginning of Israel's story instituting the festivals and ceremonies that would burn His truth into the hearts of generations of His people. He did not wait until Egypt was struck down or the Israelites were safely in the Promised Land. He gave His instructions for this first Passover, the one in Egypt, at the same moment that He gave the instructions for the Passovers that would be celebrated for all time.

Before we go further, let me make sure you know the most important truth of Passover: the true Lamb of God is Jesus Christ, the Son of the living God. This makes the Passover so thrilling to those of us in the New Covenant. In John 1:29, John the Baptist identified Jesus with these words: "Behold! The Lamb of God, who takes away the sin of the world!" (NKJV). Then, in Revelation 5:6-13, we have this description of Jesus seated at the right hand of God:

> "I saw a Lamb, looking as if it had been slain, standing at the center of the throne, encircled by the four living creatures and the elders. . . . And when he had taken it, the four living creatures and the twenty-four elders fell down before the Lamb. . . . And they sang a new song, saying:

> "'You are worthy to take the scroll and to open its seals, because you were slain, and with your blood you purchased for God persons from every tribe and language and people and nation. You have made them to be a kingdom and priests to serve our God, and they will reign on the earth.'

> "Then I looked and heard the voice of many angels, numbering thousands upon thousands, and ten thousand times ten thousand. They encircled the throne and the living creatures and the elders. In a loud voice they were saying: 'Worthy is the Lamb, who was slain, to receive power and wealth and wisdom and strength and honor and glory and praise!'

> "Then I heard every creature in heaven and on earth and under the earth and on the sea, and all that is in them, saying: 'To him who sits on the throne and to the Lamb be praise and honor and glory and power, for ever and ever!'" (NIV).

Never let us forget: Jesus is the Lamb of God! Every Passover celebrated through the centuries points to Him. Indeed, the heart of our message as Christians is that the Lamb of God has been slain for the sins of the world, and this same Lamb now reigns in heaven. Paul declared it for all time: "For Christ, our Passover lamb, has been sacrificed" (1 Corinthians 5:7, NIV).

Let me also make sure that you know my purpose in telling you about Passover. It is not just to give you historical information. My purpose is that just as the blood of the lamb was placed upon the doorposts and lintels of the Hebrew houses in Egypt, you also might be cleansed by the blood of the Lamb of God.

You see, I want us to be radical and unashamed about this matter of the blood. When God commanded that the blood should be placed on the homes of the Hebrews, He used bold terms. First, He commanded that the blood be applied with hyssop. This is a long, bushy plant that is highly aromatic.

Once dipped in the blood of the sacrifice lambs, this hyssop would apply the blood in huge swaths. We shouldn't picture little paintbrush-sized streaks of blood. No, the original Hebrew uses the word *paint* for the way the blood should be applied. It is as though our painter decided not to use brushes but bushes from our yard to paint our house. Picture big, bold, unmistakable splashes of blood.

Why is this important? The blood of the Lamb washes the sin away and leaves us protected from the curse. We shouldn't be hesitant about the blood or slow to claim its power for ourselves. Hebrews 9:22 tells us that without the shedding of blood there is no remission of sin. This is why our Savior was so horribly wounded – to shed the blood that would set us free.

Here are a few quotes from my book, *The Cross: One Man, One Tree, One Friday,* that will remind you of the excruciating suffering our Lord endured during His crucifixion, all for you and me:

> "As we stand watching, in stupefied horror, inconspicuously amid the crowd of gawkers, the Son of God – the one who spoke with such power and poetry about the way God clothes the lilies of the field with beauty – is stripped naked. He is forced to face a massive stone column and leather

straps are attached to His wrists, allowing soldiers to stretch His beloved arms that were strong enough to stop the tempestuous sea and gentle enough to hold the little children around the curve of the column and thereby stretching the skin of His back taut.

"The cursed whip consists of several strips of leather with a series of stone beads or metal balls spaced periodically along the length of each strand. At the tip of each strip is a jagged fragment of sheep bone hewn and filed sharp as a razor. The wielder of the whip is an expert in his ghastly craft – trained to inflict maximum pain and damage but without killing his victim.[13]

"Finally, and suddenly, it is over. The volume of blood now pooled around the base of the column is astonishing. His piercing eyes are now swollen shut from repeated blows from dozens of fists, beard partially yanked out at the roots, and the devastating effects of the flogging have rendered Jesus of Nazareth essentially unrecognizable. Even so, the worst is yet to come.

"The woven ring of thorns is jammed brutally down upon His hemorrhaging brow and the robe is thrown over the raw and torn flesh of His blood-soaked back. We witness another demon-inspired round of spitting, punching and taunting before the robe is ripped from his back, reopening His wounds, and is replaced by a roughhewn wooden cross beam which, in His deplorable and depleted condition, He must now carry.[14]

"We witness in anguish as Jesus is hurled to the ground and roughly stretched out upon the cross beam which had been delivered and deposited by Simon. A five-inch-long spike is struck by an anvil driving it crashing through sinews and flesh. As His nerves contort, in horrible spasms, with great precision, both nails find their marks in each wrist just

---

[13] Parsley, Rod. *The Cross: One Man…One Tree…One Friday*. Lake Mary, FL: Charisma House, 2013. Print, p. 58.
[14] Ibid, p. 59.

below the base of the hand and sink deeply into the wooden beam.

"Then, with aid of ropes and pulleys, the beam, with man attached, is hoisted up and into place atop the vertical post. The force of the beam dropping into place immediately jerks both arms out of their shoulder sockets. Jesus, our Savior, dangles there momentarily, but the Flesh Nailer has two more spikes in his hand.

"He takes hold of one of Jesus' feet and positions it, not at the front of the vertical beam but at the side. Then he drives the spike sideways, through the thickest portion of the ankle bone, and on into the post. He repeats this with the other foot on the other side of the post."[15]

I invite you to take a moment sometime soon and examine the whole text of Isaiah 53. Don't shy away from the description of Jesus being savaged and brutalized. He did it for you, so the blood He spilled could be applied to your life. This is why David, in repentance after his vile adultery, cried out to God and said, "Cleanse me with hyssop, and I will be clean; wash me, and I will be whiter than snow" (Psalm 51:7, NIV). David knew what the blood could do – even in his day, before the Son of God shed the most precious blood of all.

Even now, as you read these words, ask God to be your Passover once again. Ask Him to apply the powerful blood of Jesus in generous amounts to the mounting sin in your life. The cleansing will come. The curse will pass you by. The Lamb of God will enter your life and make you what you are meant to be in service to the living God.

The Feast of Passover

Beginning the second year after the Exodus of Israel from Egypt, the Hebrew people began celebrating the Feast of Passover. They would call it *Pesach* (PAY-sahk), the Hebrew word for "pass over." We can imagine their joy. As they wandered in the wilderness of

---

[15] Ibid, p. 70.

Sinai, they had the privilege of reenacting and celebrating their deliverance from Egypt. What a delight! This deliverance had not only freed them from bondage but also made them a people set apart for God.

It was a joyous occasion, but it was conducted with the utmost seriousness. The observance of Passover was commanded. It defined those who were and those were not members of the covenant of God. As Numbers 9:13 declared, "The man who . . . ceases to keep the Passover, that same person shall be cut off from among his people because he did not bring the offering of the LORD at its appointed time; that man shall bear his sin" (NKJV).

Passover would begin, as it had in Egypt, on the fourteenth of the first month, or Nisan. Each Hebrew family had chosen its lamb four days before then, and they knew that it was unblemished. On the sacred day, the lamb was sacrificed and cooked for the evening meal. At twilight, the Passover would begin and would proceed as God had commanded Moses at the first Passover:

> "That same night they are to eat the meat roasted over the fire, along with bitter herbs, and bread made without yeast. Do not eat the meat raw or boiled in water, but roast it over a fire – with the head, legs and internal organs. Do not leave any of it till morning; if some is left till morning, you must burn it. This is how you are to eat it: with your cloak tucked into your belt, your sandals on your feet and your staff in your hand. Eat it in haste; it is the LORD's Passover" (Exodus 12:8-11, NIV).

One of the distinctive features of the Passover meal was its educational purpose. God had instructed Moses to make sure the young were taught on this holy night of Passover:

> "When your children ask you, 'What does this ceremony mean to you?' then tell them, 'It is the Passover sacrifice to the LORD, who passed over the houses of the Israelites in Egypt and spared our homes when he struck down the Egyptians'" (Exodus 12:26, NIV).

Down through the centuries, the rabbis evolved a large body of traditions that would accompany the Passover meal and convey its meaning to all the generations present. Because this sacred meal is celebrated by families, the wife usually starts the service by lighting traditional Passover candles and by praying, "Blessed art Thou, O Lord, King of the Universe, who sanctifies us by Thy commandment and commands us to light the Lights of the Passover."

There are also dramas that members of the family play out. For example, there is a role for a wise child, a wicked child, a simple child, and a foolish child. All have speaking parts in a type of family skit. There are also object lessons drawn from the bread that is used – unleavened bread called *matzo* (MAHT-zoh) – and even from eggs, cloth, salt, and the shank of the lamb.

All of this is designed to teach the next generation the core truth of God's care for His people. The heart of this truth is surveyed in Deuteronomy 6:20-25:

> "When thy son asketh thee in time to come, saying, What mean the testimonies, and the statutes, and the judgments, which the LORD our God hath commanded you? Then thou shalt say unto thy son, We were Pharaoh's bondmen in Egypt; and the LORD brought us out of Egypt with a mighty hand:

> "And the LORD shewed signs and wonders, great and sore, upon Egypt, upon Pharaoh, and upon all his household, before our eyes: and he brought us out from thence, that he might bring us in, to give us the land which he sware unto our fathers.

> "And the LORD commanded us to do all these statutes, to fear the LORD our God, for our good always, that he might preserve us alive, as it is at this day. And it shall be our righteousness, if we observe to do all these commandments before the LORD our God, as he hath commanded us."

One of the most important traditions that evolved around the Passover meal has to do with cups of wine. This is important to us because it is a tradition that Jesus used to explain to His disciples and the world the meaning of His sacrifice.

We must remember that what we Christians call the Last Supper was for Jesus and His disciples a Passover meal. Our Jewish friends call this meal a *Seder* (SAY-duhr), which means "order" or "arrangement." This sacred meal has evolved through the centuries for the observance of the Passover feast.

Well before the day of Jesus, a practice had evolved of using four cups of wine as symbols of God's provision. This ritual was designed to celebrate the promises of Exodus 6:6-7:

> "Say unto the children of Israel, I am the LORD, and I will bring you out from under the burdens of the Egyptians, and I will rid you out of their bondage, and I will redeem you with a stretched out arm, and with great judgments: And I will take you to me for a people, and I will be to you a God: and ye shall know that I am the LORD your God, which bringeth you out from under the burdens of the Egyptians."

Four "I will" statements are in these verses. The practice of the four cups of wine was intended by the rabbis to allow celebrants to honor God for each of four promises made in this passage from Exodus.

The first cup of wine is known as the Cup of Consecration. It celebrated the truth of "I will bring you out." When His people were in Egypt, God remembered their bondage. He visited the plagues upon Egypt in judgment. He then parted the Red Sea as He took Israel out of her slavery. These words live in the mind of a Jew: "God brought us out. Let us consecrate ourselves to Him." The first cup of wine is consumed in celebration of the tremendous mercy of God, a mercy that calls for sanctification.

The second cup of wine is known as the Cup of Deliverance. It is based on the promise "I will free you from bondage." This cup did not merely celebrate that God had removed His people from Egypt, but that the spirit of Egypt and the ways of Egypt were also removed from the hearts of God's people. This is the complement to the Cup of Consecration. This is the declaration that deliverance is complete. Israel is delivered from Egypt, but Egypt is also taken out of Israel.

The third cup of wine is the Cup of Redemption. This cup is used to celebrate the promise "I will redeem you." This meant that God would pay any price to stretch out His arm, destroy all enemies, and make Israel His people. The emphasis here is upon an act of redemption, the act of paying a price to deliver or rescue. God would stop at nothing to make Israel His own.

There is a fourth cup of wine, but we will wait a moment to consider it. What is surprising about the Last Supper, which was a Passover meal, is that Jesus paused during this traditional four-cup progression and used the third cup to reveal what was about to happen.

In Luke 22:20, we are told that as Jesus sat at the table of the Passover meal, He took this third cup into His hand and said, "This cup is the new testament in my blood, which is shed for you."

Think of it. For centuries God's people had celebrated Passover. For centuries they had eaten lamb with bitter herbs and remembered their national birth in the deliverance from Egypt. And for centuries, they had consumed four cups of wine in honor of God's great provision as described in Exodus 6.

Yet on this sacred night, the night of the last Passover Jesus would ever celebrate during His life on earth, our Lord took the third cup of wine and declared Himself the fulfillment of its meaning.

Yes, He was saying, *our heavenly Father will spare no expense to fashion a people of His own. You drink a cup of wine every year in celebration of this promise. Yet I now tell you that the Father is paying the final price. He's paying it in the blood of His Son. The cup you hold in your hand, this Cup of Redemption, is actually the cup of a New Covenant to be purchased with my blood. All of this is done graciously by the heavenly Father for you.*

Our heavenly Father will spare no expense to fashion a people of His own.

This truth echoes through the ages. Jesus is the Passover. He is the Lamb of God. His blood is the once and for all sacrifice that makes all other sacrifices obsolete. His blood redeems. His blood cleanses. His blood makes right what has been destroyed through sin. Drink the cup of His blood and be liberated by the living God, just as the children of Israel were liberated in Egypt of old.

A beautiful picture arises from the rabbinic tradition of these four cups. In the record of the teachings of the ancient rabbis, which is called the *Mishnah*, (MEESH-nah) we are told "the Passover wine was said to be red and was to be mixed with warm water."[16] Ask a rabbi why wine and warm water were mixed, and he will tell you that this mixture of blood and water produces a closer representation of the blood of the Passover Lamb.

This ancient tradition begs us to remember that tragic day when the perfect and precious Lamb of God was sacrificed. There came a moment after Jesus had hung on that rugged rail for six excruciating hours. He had just uttered the sacred words, "It is finished," and Mary, his mother, who watched Him take His first breath, wept as He exhaled His last, thus completing His Father's master plan to redeem this cursed planet and the souls of men.

Once again I am compelled to quote from *The Cross: One Man, One Tree, One Friday*, regarding that powerful and prophetic statement, "It is finished." We need to understand a specific term:

> "When John, the beloved disciple, recalls this statement to record it in his gospel narrative, he uses a Greek accounting term – *tetelestai*. Future English translations of John's gospel will render that term in a way that tends to strip it of the legal and financial connotations.

> "They translate it, 'It is finished' (three words for one). But *tetelestai* does not mean merely that a thing has ended. It has a far greater implication than merely a clock has run out and the game has concluded. It is a declaration that all has been accomplished.

---

[16] Pesahim 7:13.

"All that was lacking has now been supplied. The breach has been healed. The debt has been fully satisfied. Shalom – nothing broken, nothing missing."[17]

We are told in John 19:33-34 that when the Roman soldiers approached the body of Jesus, they "saw that he was dead already, they brake not his legs: But one of the soldiers with a spear pierced his side, and forthwith came there out blood and water."

Think of it. All through the centuries God's covenant people drank a ceremonial cup of wine mixed with water and called it a "Cup of Redemption." Jesus, the sinless Lamb of God, offers Himself upon a cross as the final sacrifice, and then out of His dead body pour blood and water together. For centuries Passovers had foreshadowed what those who celebrated them never could have conceived. Jesus, the sinless Lamb of God, was the final Passover sacrifice.

And what of that fourth cup of wine? It was the Cup of Praise. The Hebrew word for "praise" is *hallel* (hah-LEHL), and so this cup is often referred to even in English as the "Cup of Hallel." It was the cup consumed in honor of God's promise, "I will take you to me for a people."

Yet Jesus did not drink this cup on that final Passover of His earthly life. After drinking the third cup at that Last Supper, Jesus and His disciples rose, sang a hymn, and made their way to the Garden of Gethsemane. The fourth cup of wine, this Cup of Praise, sat on the table in the Upper Room while Jesus went out into the night.

What should this mean to us? This fourth cup is the cup of the Marriage Feast. Remember its theme? "I will take you to me for a people." It is the cup to be consumed when Jesus takes His Bride and the wedding celebration of the Lamb commences. Jesus was referring to this cup when He said:

"This is my blood of the new testament, which is shed for many for the remission of sins. But I say unto you, I will not drink henceforth of this fruit of the vine, until that day when

---

[17] Parsley, Rod. *The Cross: One Man...One Tree...One Friday*. Lake Mary, FL: Charisma House, 2013. Print, p. 90.

I drink it new with you in my Father's kingdom" (Matthew 26:28-29).

A party awaits us. It is the grand ball that will begin when Jesus comes for His church, His Bride without spot or wrinkle, and takes her for His own. He's already paid the price. What remains is for the wedding of the Lamb and His Bride. On that day, we will all drink that fourth Cup of Praise (Hallel) in the Kingdom of God. And we will dance. Oh, how we will dance!

Pesach Sheni

Now let me tell you about an aspect of the Passover festival that has the power to change you forever but is rarely taught in our churches. It will help you walk in the majesty of Passover more fully, and it will also prepare you for understanding the Feast of Unleavened Bread that follows the day of Passover.

We learn about this surprising part of Passover in the book of Numbers. It arises from an important moment during the second year after Israel came out of Egypt and just as it was time to celebrate the Passover. Of course, that means it was Nisan, the first month. God reminded Moses it was time to celebrate the Passover. Moses in turn commanded the people, and the Bible tells us that "the Israelites did everything just as the LORD commanded Moses" (Numbers 9:5, NIV).

Then a troubling question arose. It turned out that some of the Israelites had recently handled a dead body. Under the law this made them ceremonially unclean, which meant that they could not partake of the Passover. They took this problem – it was a complaint, really – to Moses. "Should we be kept from the Lord's Passover?" these men asked.

Now Moses, who the Bible tells us was a humble man, didn't know the answer for this problem. So he told the people to wait while he sought the Lord. When Moses returned, he told the people the following:

"When any of you or your descendants are unclean because of a dead body or are away on a journey, they are still to celebrate the LORD's Passover, but they are to do it on the fourteenth day of the second month at twilight. They are to eat the lamb, together with unleavened bread and bitter herbs.

"They must not leave any of it till morning or break any of its bones. When they celebrate the Passover, they must follow all the regulations. But if anyone who is ceremonially unclean, and not on a journey fails to celebrate the Passover, they must be cut off from their people for not presenting the LORD's offering at the appointed time. They will bear the consequences of their sin" (Numbers 9:10-13, NIV).

This commandment created a second Passover possibility. The Hebrew for this is *Pesach Sheni* (PAY-sahk- SHAY-nee), which literally means "second Passover." One month after the official Passover, which as we know occurred on the fourteenth of Nisan, there could be a second Passover, which would land on the fourteenth of the second month or Iyar. This second Passover was for those who were away from the land on a journey or who were ritually unclean when the Passover of the first month occurred.

This second Passover was just like the first Passover in most ways. The people who celebrated were to eat roasted lamb with bitter herbs. They were to eat it in haste and with their cloaks tucked in, their sandals on their feet, and their staffs in their hands. All of this had been commanded. Yet there was one major difference, and it brings us to the subject of leaven. I've waited until now to describe this because it is such a vital part of understanding Pesach Sheni and what it means for you.

A primary feature of Passover was God's command that the people should eat no yeast as part of their meal. They were to eat only bread without yeast or unleavened bread, "That same night they are to eat the meat roasted over the fire, along with bitter herbs, and bread made without yeast" (Exodus 12:8, NIV).

Why no yeast? In Scripture, leaven is a symbol of sin. It is actually a perfect symbol. Leaven makes bread rise. It puffs up. It lives and grows and ferments – and corrupts. It is a perfect picture of what sin does. So, from the beginning, God dealt with His people about leaven in their food or in their homes almost as though it was sin itself. He was using a natural object to teach a spiritual lesson.

From time to time He commanded them not to eat leaven or even have it in their homes as a way of saying that they also ought to separate themselves from the sin that leaven symbolized.

So, on the night of Passover, the people were to eat unleavened bread as a symbol of a life without sin. The next feast after Passover, as we'll see in a moment, was an entire week devoted to removing leaven – and sin – from their lives.

However what is interesting about this second Passover, Pesach Sheni, is that it did not have the same restrictions about leaven. But why? If leaven is so horrible – if it is sin and it puffs up and if it is the perfect symbol of the wicked, puffed up pride that has destroyed mankind – then surely it should be as banned on the second Passover as it is on the first.

Not so. There are no restrictions about leaven being present when it comes to Pesach Sheni, the second Passover. Many Jewish sages say that it is even permissible to eat leaven with your matzo, your unleavened bread, and with your Passover lamb. In any case, whether you may consume it at the exact moment that you consume the Passover lamb or not is a bit debatable, but what is not debatable is there is no prohibition of having leaven in your home.

There's no restriction against owning leaven or even having leaven at your Passover table. One can eat the matzo or the unleavened bread, and one can take that swallow and, with the very next bite, take a piece of leavened bread and consume that with the Passover lamb. There's no prohibition whatsoever when it comes to this Pesach Sheni.

This is stunning. And I ask again, why is this so? If I missed out on the first Passover, shouldn't the same standards apply to the second? Shouldn't I observe the same lesson about the wickedness of leaven?

It would make sense, but hear me: God is speaking a mystery to us through the ancients. Leaven represents the human ego, self-will, and self-assertion.

In the first Passover, God is saying *get rid of the leaven, get rid of your ego, get rid of your self, get rid of your self-will*. In the second Passover, He is reminding us that our salvation is of Him and not of us. He's teaching us in one symbol what Martin Luther bled to learn and generations have been bound up spiritually for forgetting. It is this: salvation is from the Lord. We didn't find the Lord. We didn't save ourselves. We can't get to heaven by conquering our sins in our own strength. It isn't as easy as getting some containers of yeast out of your house.

Get rid of the leaven, get rid of your ego, get rid of your self, get rid of your self will.

No, you can't save yourself. You didn't find the Lord. You didn't know where to look for Him. Instead, out of the swirling ages of eternity past, He came looking for you – treading the earthly way, heaven come down, God incarnate, knocking on your heart. No man comes to God unless the Spirit draws him.

In short, this Pesach Sheni, this second Passover, is about grace. It is about the fact that Jesus found me. He claimed me. He saved me. He washed me. He made me His own. I never could have saved myself. I never could have put the leaven out of my life as an act of my will. No, I'm saved because God granted His grace, the same kind of grace we see in Pesach Sheni when the ban against leaven is lifted.

Let me say this another way. Here's what Passover says to the Jew: "You had no more to do with being a Jew than you had to do with being born. So, how could you come with arrogance? How could you come with ego? You are a Jew because God reached down and delivered you by His mighty hand and made you His own. He made you a people for Himself."

This is the message of Passover. For a Christian, the message, particularly of this Pesach Sheni, is much the same. I didn't decide when I would come into relationship with Jesus. I was in darkness. I was a stranger. I was an alien to the Commonwealth of Israel. I was a stranger to the covenants of promise. They didn't make any sense to me.

Yet, right there in my mess, right there in my depravity, He came all the way down. He identified with me. He laid His hand on my mouth and sanctified my lips. He put His hand on my heart. He took out a stony heart and put in a heart of flesh so I could serve Him. I am His because He chose me. I got picked. I got adopted. I wasn't a part of this family. I didn't have the right bloodline, but I got adopted. He came to the dog pound of humanity and saw me and said, "That's the one I want."

It is by grace we are saved. We did not choose Jesus; He chose us. The two Passovers show us both the righteous standard of God – no leaven shall be among you in the first Passover – and the mystery of grace – even if there is leaven, God will save you anyway. How grateful we ought to be.

So you see that from the first feast in the first month at the beginning of the Hebrew calendar, God was doing miracles on earth and in history, but He commanded that they be commemorated in a way that prefigured Jesus. He wanted Passover celebrated with lamb's blood, unleavened bread, bitter herbs, and wine.

He wanted a second Passover for the unclean where the standards weren't as high, but the grace was as deep. He wanted all this celebrated every year, so that the liberation of God might be declared before the nations of the world.

The message would be, "Here is the Passover of God. Come under the blood. Come free of the sin. Come into the mercy. The judgment and the destruction can pass you by."

The Feast of Unleavened Bread

We must remember that technically Passover is a single day. It is one day of deliverance. It is one meal consumed on one night that radiates its meaning throughout the year.

The day after Passover, though, begins a separate but related feast; God calls it the Feast of Unleavened Bread. In Hebrew this is *Chag HaMatzoht* (khahg hah-maht-ZOHT). At the same time that God gave Moses his instructions for the first Passover while Israel was still in Egypt, He gave instructions for this Feast of Unleavened Bread:

> "Celebrate the Festival of Unleavened Bread, because it was on this very day that I brought your divisions out of Egypt. Celebrate this day as a lasting ordinance for the generations to come. In the first month, you are to eat bread made without yeast, from the evening of the fourteenth day until the evening of the twenty-first day.
>
> "For seven days no yeast is to be found in your houses. And anyone, whether foreigner or native-born, who eats anything with yeast in it must be cut off from the community of Israel. Eat nothing made with yeast. Where you live, you must eat unleavened bread" (Exodus 12:17-20, NIV).

Let me remind you of the importance of yeast before we consider in some detail this festival entirely devoted to the removal of yeast. Remember that leaven is a metaphor for sin in the Bible. It is the hidden corruption, the undetected cancer of sin that dwells within us. It is a corrupting force that works unseen and unheard.

This yeast or leaven, which in Hebrew is called *chametz* (khah-METZ), is just like sin in that it goes to work out of sight to raise up, to puff up, and to lift itself up. It is a living, breathing thing that has the purpose of exalting, and it does so by feeding itself from the organism it invades and then breeding until it controls that organism. This is a perfect illustration of what sin does.

Beginning with the Feast of Passover, God desired to illustrate how far His people must remove leaven/sin from their lives. He commanded them on that first Passover to eat only unleavened bread. Nearly in the same breath, He commanded that the next day the people should begin observing this Feast of Unleavened Bread, a week in which no leaven should be eaten or even be present in their homes.

This led to an astonishing scene pregnant with meaning for us. On the day after that first Passover in Egypt, the fifteenth of Nisan, the people of God awoke and prepared to do as God commanded: eat only bread without yeast – unleavened bread. Yet the Hebrew people had no chance to finish their baking because the Egyptians hurried them out of the land. Exodus 12:33-34 tells us:

"The Egyptians urged the people, that they might send them out of the land in haste. For they said, 'We shall all be dead.' So the people took their dough before it was leavened, having their kneading bowls bound up in their clothes on their shoulders" (NKJV).

Imagine the scene. Two or three million people marched out of Egypt carrying unleavened dough in their hands and kneading bowls bound up in their clothes and bags. The lesson is clear. None of the leaven of Egypt was to go with the Jews to their Promised Land.

God did not want to merely remove the Hebrews from Egypt. He wanted to remove the spirit and practices of Egypt – the sinful ways of Egypt – from the hearts of His people. It's as though we can hear the ancient words of Isaiah ringing in our ears as we picture the Israelites leaving Egypt with their bread and their bread bowls in their hands:

"Depart! Depart! Go out from there, Touch no unclean thing; Go out from the midst of her, Be clean, You who bear the vessels of the LORD" (Isaiah 52:11, NKJV).

The Feast of Unleavened Bread imprinted these lessons into the hearts of God's people through the centuries. In the Jewish tradition, the entire month before Passover was used to remove all leaven from every home. Even today during the weeks prior to Passover, Jewish families use the Internet and other methods to sell anything they own that has leaven in it.

This is very much like a festival of repentance and renewal, in which anything sinful or corrupting is removed. This is what the Feast of Unleavened Bread symbolizes. When the feast begins on the day after Pentecost, homes swept clean of leaven serve only unleavened bread or *matzo*. During this feast, no work is done, and burnt sacrifices are made.

In God's instructions for the Feast of Unleavened Bread, the emphasis is upon total separation from Egypt. To use another biblical metaphor, it is as though the people of God are to "shake the dust" of Egypt off themselves, as though they are to have not even the tiniest spore of yeast among them that could one day lead to corruption and destruction. Listen to the terms God uses to explain His feast and command what should be taught regarding it to the next generation:

> "You shall observe the Feast of Unleavened Bread, for on this same day I will have brought your armies out of the land of Egypt" (Exodus 12:17, NKJV).

> "Unleavened bread shall be eaten seven days. And no leavened bread shall be seen among you, nor shall leaven be seen among you in all your quarters. And you shall tell your son in that day, saying, 'This is done because of what the LORD did for me when I came up from Egypt.'

> "It shall be as a sign to you on your hand as a memorial between your eyes, that the Lord's law may be in your mouth; for with a strong hand the LORD has brought you out of Egypt" (Exodus 13:7-9, NKJV).

The powerful meaning of this Feast of Unleavened Bread was often on the Apostle Paul's mind as he urged the young Christian church to holiness. The early church was largely Jewish, so Paul's audience knew what he referred to when he wrote in 1 Corinthians 5:6, "Your glorying is not good. Know ye not that a little leaven leaveneth the whole lump?"

Keep in mind that most of the young Christians who heard these words had observed Passover and the Feast of Unleavened Bread their whole lives. From childhood they had participated in the search for leaven in their homes.

Since birth they had eaten the Passover meal using matzo bread without yeast, and then they had observed an entire week in which there could be no yeast in their lives in any form. When Paul warned them about a little leaven permeating the whole lump, nearly every member of the New Testament church knew the power of what he said. Yet Paul was not just urging the people of the early church to remove the leaven of sin from their lives. He was also urging them to eat the pure bread of Jesus Christ:

> "Purge out therefore the old leaven, that ye may be a new lump, as ye are unleavened. For even Christ our passover is sacrificed for us: Therefore let us keep the feast, not with old leaven, neither with the leaven of malice and wickedness;

but with the unleavened bread of sincerity and truth" (1 Corinthians 5:7-8).

Paul wanted his largely Jewish audience in the early church to understand that salvation does not come by removing sin through human effort. No, salvation comes by eating the bread of Jesus Christ. Just consider how far God went to reveal Jesus as the unleavened bread of God, the fulfillment of all references to unleavened bread throughout biblical history. Jesus is described as "the Bread of Life." He was born in Bethlehem, which in Hebrew means "House of Bread." He often used bread as an image of Himself: "Unless a kernel of wheat falls to the ground . . ." (John 12:24, NIV). The truth He preached is called the "Bread of Life."

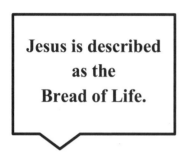

Jesus is described as the Bread of Life.

Even the matzo bread used at Passover and at the Feast of Unleavened Bread alluded to Him. Perhaps you've seen this bread. It is striped ("With his stripes we are healed" [Isaiah 53:5]), pierced ("They shall look on him whom they pierced" [John 19:37]), and pure – without any leaven – as the body of Jesus is pure and without any sin.

What resulted from this life free of leaven or sin? What happened when God's people ate the pure bread of Jesus and kept their lives free of the hidden corruption of sin in their lives? Let me tell you: victory. Absolute, miraculous victory in God. You see, some might conclude that the Feast of Unleavened Bread was a bit boring.

It might be easy to think that it was a week in which God's people just didn't eat a certain kind of bread. Not too exciting, some would say. But let me tell you how misguided this thinking is. It was while the people of God in Egypt swept their homes of leaven and ate only unleavened bread that God delivered them.

It was while they made themselves clean that God acted on their behalf. Let's remember our Hebrew calendar to understand this. The first Passover took place on the fourteenth of Nisan, as all biblical Passover celebrations do. The evening of Passover began the Feast of Unleavened Bread. So the first day of Unleavened Bread was the fifteenth of Nisan, the day after Passover. Now remember that on this same day the people of God rose up and left Egypt.

Do you recall that the Hebrew people couldn't even finish baking their bread on this first day after Passover? Remember that the Egyptians were so horrified by the deaths of their firstborn that they urged the Hebrews out of the land while giving them gold and silver and other valuable things. So deliverance came for God's people on the first day of the Feast of Unleavened Bread, the fifteenth.

But that's not all. The ancient rabbis tell us that it was during the Feast of Unleavened Bread that the Israelites passed through the Red Sea on dry ground as they trekked into the wilderness of Sinai. This means it was also at that time that the army of Egypt pursued the people of God, passed into the divided Red Sea, and was destroyed when God caused the waters to flow again, drowning all of the soldiers while Israel stood and watched on dry land.

Do you see the power? The Feast of Unleavened Bread is not just a wimpy week of eating light. No! It is a time when God's people remove all evil from their lives and then stand fast to see the salvation of God. During that first Feast of Unleavened Bread, the Israelites left their 430-year bondage, had their enemy make them wealthy, marched through barriers that God removed, and then saw their enemies destroyed before their eyes.

This is the power of this feast. This is how God responds to a people who make themselves clean before Him. This is what it means to clean out the old leaven and to eat the unleavened bread of sincerity and truth. It was the way God's people prepared themselves for the victories that God destined for them.

When I think of this powerful feast, I'm reminded of the words of the Apostle Peter in Acts. Standing at one of the gates to the Temple in Jerusalem, having just healed a lame man, Peter turned to his mostly Jewish audience and said, "Repent, then, and turn to God, so that your sins may be wiped out, that times of refreshing may come from the Lord" (Acts 3:19, NIV).

I see in this verse the same themes I see in the Feast of Unleavened Bread. *If you will repent and turn to God, removing sin from your life, then God will do magnificent things for you.*

It will help you to understand the power of this promise if you know that the Greek word for "refreshing" does not just refer to a bit of inspiration or energy. It doesn't just mean a little bit of encouragement. It is a legal term used in Greek and Roman courts of law. The word actually means "the restoration of what has been stolen."

So when we repent, when we remove the leaven of sin from our lives and turn to God, He begins to restore what has been stolen from us. He begins to set us free, destroy our enemies, prosper us, and set us on our destined path. This is the great meaning of the Feast of Unleavened Bread: "Stand still and see the salvation of the LORD" (2 Chronicles 20:17, NKJV).

The Feast of Firstfruits

The theme of victory we see in the celebration of the Feast of Unleavened Bread continues in the third of the three feasts that are part of the Passover celebration. It is called the Feast of Firstfruits, which in Hebrew is called *Reshit Katzir* (reh-sheet kaht-ZEER) or "the beginning of the harvest."

The Feast of Firstfruits is exciting because it is a celebration that took place only after the people of God entered the Promised Land. When they began to prosper, God wanted them to take the first part of their harvest and offer it to Him. Consider His instructions for this feast:

> "The LORD said to Moses, 'Speak to the Israelites and say to them: 'When you enter the land I am going to give you and you reap its harvest, bring to the priest a sheaf of the first grain you harvest. He is to wave the sheaf before the LORD so it will be accepted on your behalf; the priest is to wave it on the day after the Sabbath.

> "On the day you wave the sheaf, you must sacrifice as a burnt offering to the LORD a lamb a year old without defect, together with its grain offering of the two-tenths of an ephah of the finest flour mixed with olive oil – a food offering presented to the LORD, a pleasing aroma – and its drink offering

of a quarter of a hin of wine. You must not eat any bread, or roasted or new grain, until the very day you bring this offering to your God. This is to be a lasting ordinance for the generations to come, wherever you live'" (Leviticus 23:9-14, NIV).

This feast was unique for many reasons, and one of the most important is that it took place on the first day of the week. God told Moses that this feast should be celebrated on the day after the Sabbath that occurred during the Feast of Unleavened Bread.

Since the Feast of Unleavened Bread lasted a week, one of the seven days of that feast was sure to be a Sabbath. God chose the day after this special Sabbath to be the Feast of Firstfruits. You already realize, I'm sure, that this means that Firstfruits has always fallen and will always fall on a Sunday.

The Lord established this day as a sacred *mo'edim* during which His people could celebrate the richness of the land He provided for them. They would do this by taking the very first grain of their harvest to a priest. There would be no further harvesting or consuming of the harvest until this was done. This first sheaf of grain, which in Hebrew is called an *omer* (OH-mer), was taken to the priest, who would wave this sheaf to the north, south, east, and west as a blessing of the harvest and a blessing of the land. Then a lamb without blemish would be sacrificed before the Lord.

Think about it. For 430 years the children of Israel lived in bondage in Egypt. Then, in 1446 BC, they were delivered, but they ended

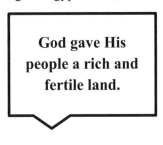

God gave His people a rich and fertile land.

up wandering for forty years in the desert of Sinai. Finally, they entered the Promised Land. Then they could plant and harvest. They could reap a full and abundant harvest because God gave His people a rich and fertile land. One omer or sheaf of grain was harvested, and God's command was that the people stop and harvest no more. Instead, they were to take that first omer and go to the priest.

They prayed a prayer of thanksgiving for all that God had done. Then the priest took the sheaf and waved it over the land. The actions had symbolic meaning: *May this blessing continue. May this bounty continue throughout the land. May this land continue to grant a great harvest for generations to come.* Then an unblemished lamb was sacrificed, an offering to our generous and faithful God.

We receive deeper understanding of God's will for this feast when we read the words that God gave Moses. In this restatement of the commandments for the Feast of Firstfruits, God describes a confession that His people should make, one that honors God and reminds the people of what He has done:

"When you have entered the land the LORD your God is giving you as an inheritance and have taken possession of it and settled in it, take some of the firstfruits of all that you produce from the soil of the land the LORD your God is giving you and put them in a basket.

"Then go to the place the LORD your God will choose as a dwelling for his Name and say to the priest in office at the time, 'I declare today to the LORD your God that I have come to the land the LORD swore to our ancestors to give us.' The priest shall take the basket from your hands and set it down in front of the altar of the LORD your God.

"Then you shall declare before the LORD your God: 'My father was a wandering Aramean, and he went down into Egypt with a few people and lived there and became a great nation, powerful and numerous. But the Egyptians mistreated us and made us suffer, subjecting us to harsh labor. Then we cried out to the LORD, the God of our ancestors, and the LORD heard our voice and saw our misery, toil and oppression. So the LORD brought us out of Egypt with a mighty hand and an outstretched arm, with great terror and with signs and wonders.

"'He brought us to this place and gave us this land, a land flowing with milk and honey; and now I bring the firstfruits of the soil that you, LORD, have given me.' Place the basket before the LORD your God and bow down before him. Then you and the Levites and the foreigners residing among you

69

shall rejoice in all the good things the LORD your God has given to you and your household" (Deuteronomy 26:1-11, NIV).

What a thrilling moment that must have been for God's people! After so much torment and so many years of oppression, finally they are in their land, harvesting its great abundance and giving thanks to God for everything.

You can see how God's three Spring Feasts form a unity. The Feast of Passover is the celebration of redemption. God "passed over" the houses of the Hebrews in Egypt and set His people free. The Feast of Unleavened Bread is a remembrance of the call to be free of sin and a celebration of the deliverance that comes to a holy people. God took the Hebrews out of Egypt, carried them through the Red Sea, and destroyed their enemies during this feast. Then God took the people into the Promised Land, a land rich and abundant – "flowing with milk and honey" (Exodus 3:8, NIV).

During their first harvest in that new land, He commanded that they stop and honor Him for His blessings. This is the Feast of Firstfruits. It is the celebration that God has brought His people into a fertile land and blessed them, that God has completed the deliverance of His people. That this feast takes place on a Sunday ought to be a signal to us. It shouldn't take long for us to realize that the Sunday of Firstfruits is the same day that Jesus Christ our Lord was raised from the dead. We are used to calling this Sunday "Easter," but our Lord was raised from the dead on the Feast of Firstfruits. Look at the progression of His final week, "Passion Week" we sometimes call it, as it relates to the feasts of God.

Nisan 14: We know that this is the date of the Jewish Passover, and we know that Jesus celebrated His Passover meal or *Seder* on this night with His disciples.

Nisan 15: This was the Sabbath, and on this day Jesus lay in the tomb. Since this is the day after Passover, it was also the first day of the Feast of Unleavened Bread.

Nisan 16: Jesus was raised from the dead, on the Sunday after the Sabbath during the Feast of the Unleavened Bread.

Now, this truth – that Jesus was raised from the dead on the Feast of Firstfruits – is thrilling to us, since we now understand what this feast is. Listen to what Paul said about it:

"Christ has indeed been raised from the dead, the firstfruits of those who have fallen asleep. For since death came through a man, the resurrection of the dead comes also through a man.

"For as in Adam all die, so in Christ all will be made alive. But each in turn: Christ, the firstfruits; then, when he comes, those who belong to him" (1 Corinthians 15:20-23, NIV).

Just picture the scene that unfolded on the day that Jesus was raised. It is Sunday, the first day of the week. The Sabbath day was the day before, and it was the Sabbath during the Feast of Unleavened Bread. It was also the Sabbath after Passover.

Now, on this Sunday morning, women rush to the tomb where Jesus was buried. They are carrying spices and fragrant oils with which to dress the body of Jesus. They were not able to finish the job when Jesus was buried because the sun was setting on that Friday.

The Sabbath was beginning, and it was against the law to move about the city. So they have returned now on this Sunday morning to finish the job of tending the horribly marred body of Jesus. As they walk to the grave, smoke ascends from the Temple; an unblemished lamb is being sacrificed. This is a special sacrifice

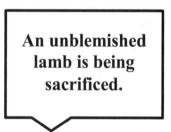

An unblemished lamb is being sacrificed.

for the day that God ordained for the Feast of Firstfruits. The priests at the Temple are doing what priests have done on this day for generations.

As the women arrive at the garden tomb, they discover that Jesus is not there. They are told, "He has risen." And though they might not have understood it then, Jesus had become the firstfruits for all mankind. Through Him, God delivered all men willing to believe and brought them into a rich and abundant Promised Land of the Kingdom of God. Jesus, our Firstfruits, was raised from the dead.

What does this Feast of Firstfruits mean to you? It means that in Jesus Christ, as a result of His grace in your life through faith, you have entered into your Promised Land. Hear this: Jesus Christ is your Promised Land.

Your years of oppression and rebellious wandering have ended. Now you can begin to enjoy seed time and harvest time in the Kingdom of God; you can begin to reap the glorious riches that have been provided by our Lord. Never forget that Firstfruits means that we ought always to live in gratitude, in tearful acknowledgment of God's grace, and in humble recognition that we were lost but now we are found, delivered, planted, and set upon the path of an abundant life in Jesus.

The Feast of Weeks

The fourth feast of the seven major feasts of God has a number of names. In Hebrew, it is called *Shavuot* (sha-voo-OHT), which means "weeks." As a result, in English this feast is often called "the Feast of Weeks," yet we know it better as "the Feast of Pentecost."

Many of our Jewish friends use yet another name for this feast: *Atzeret Pesach* (aht-ZEH-reht PAY-sahk). It means "Conclusion of Pentecost." Even though the Feast of Weeks is not one of the three feasts most associated with Passover – Passover, Unleavened Bread, and Firstfruits – it is still a conclusion of at least the first stage in the creation of a people of God.

In Leviticus 23, the Magna Carta chapter of the feasts of God, the commandments regarding this Feast of Weeks are very specific:

"From the day after the Sabbath, the day you brought the sheaf of the wave offering, count off seven full weeks. Count off fifty days up to the day after the seventh Sabbath, and then present an offering of new grain to the LORD.

"From where you live, bring two loaves made of two-tenths of an ephah of the finest flour, baked with yeast, as a wave offering of firstfruits to the LORD.

"Present with this bread seven male lambs, each a year old and without defect, one young bull and two rams. They will be a burnt offering to the LORD, together with their grain offerings and drink offerings – a food offering, an aroma pleasing to the LORD. Then sacrifice one male goat for a sin offering and two lambs, each a year old, for a fellowship offering. The priest is to wave the two lambs before the LORD as a wave offering, together with the bread of the firstfruits. They are a sacred offering to the LORD for the priest.

"On that same day, you are to proclaim a sacred assembly and do no regular work. This is to be a lasting ordinance for the generations to come, wherever you live. When you reap the harvest of your land, do not reap to the very edges of your field or gather the gleanings of your harvest. Leave them for the poor and for the foreigner residing among you. I am the LORD your God" (Leviticus 23:15-22, NIV).

The opening words of these commands remind us that God is a God of exact timing and defined seasons. He makes it clear that He wants this fourth feast to take place exactly fifty days or seven weeks and a day after the Feast of Firstfruits. Again, this is why this festival is usually called simply "Weeks." It's interesting to note, the word *Pentecost* by which we Christians usually refer to this festival is the Greek word for "fiftieth day." So both the Greek and the Hebrew words for this festival come from the period of time – fifty days or seven weeks and a day – between the Feast of Firstfruits and the Feast of Weeks.

This gap between these two feasts is so significant that Jewish tradition has given it a name and a ceremony of its own. The fifty days between Firstfruits and Weeks are called *Sefirat HaOmer* (SEH-fih-raht hah-OH-mer) in Hebrew, or the "Counting of the Omer." Remember that the word *omer* means "sheaf." So on each day between these two feasts – and both take place during the spring harvest season – the sheaves of grain were counted and celebrated.

All of this was a grand celebration of the bounty of the Lord, a rejoicing in the harvest that was much like an extension of the gratitude and joy that attended Firstfruits. Each evening, after the omers were counted but before the number was announced, the chief rabbi recited the following blessing:

Blessed are you, O Lord our God, King of the universe,
Who by His command to count the omer has sanctified us.

Then Jewish tradition required the reciting of Psalm 67. This psalm is composed of forty-nine Hebrew words, the same as the number of days ordained for counting the omer.

"May God be gracious to us and bless us and make his face shine on us – so that your ways may be known on earth, your salvation among all nations.

"May the peoples praise you, God; may all the peoples praise you. May the nations be glad and sing for joy, for you rule the people with equity and guide the nations of the earth. May the peoples praise you, God; may all the peoples praise you.

"The land yields its harvest; God, our God, blesses us. May God bless us still, so that all the ends of the earth will fear him" (NIV).

By the time the Feast of Weeks arrived, the people were filled with joy. They had begun celebrating the goodness of God fifty days before at Firstfruits. Then they counted God's bounty every day and recited psalms in praise of His generosity: "The land yields its harvest; God, our God, blesses us." Then the Feast of Weeks arrived, a time in which the bounty of the later harvest season was celebrated.

But this Feast of Weeks is far more than another celebration of a rich harvest. It is also a celebration of the giving of the Torah – the law and revelation of God – to His people. To understand this, we have to understand how the sages have dated certain events in Jewish history.

According to rabbinic tradition, the Feast of Weeks occurred on the same day of the year that Moses gave the Torah to the people. This is based on Exodus 19:1, "In the third month after the children of Israel had gone out of the land of Egypt, on the same day, they came to the Wilderness of Sinai" (NKJV). So, Israel left Egypt on the fifteenth of the first month.

Forty-five days later the people arrived at Mount Sinai. Then Moses went up the holy mountain for one day, and three days of preparation followed. After these three days, the covenant was sealed in blood, and the people went up the mountain with Moses to meet with God. This means fifty days in all.

Now before you and I understood something about the Hebrew calendar, we might have missed this meaning of the Feast of Weeks. Our Jewish friends, though, particularly the ancient rabbis, knew immediately that this festival was intended to celebrate the giving of the Torah.

They knew what we now know: our God is a God of times and dates, of symbols and patterns. He wanted His people to celebrate the latter part of the harvest, yes, but He also wanted them to remember the date He gave the Torah and celebrate it as well.

This is precisely why the Feast of Weeks is sometimes known as *Atzeret Pesach* (aht-ZEH-reht PAY-sahk), the "Conclusion of Passover." Why did God deliver the Israelites out of Egypt? To make them a people for Himself; to make them a people of His will and His ways.

So God gave the Israelites the pillar of fire by day and the pillar of fire by night. He gave them His feasts, and He gave them an anointed leader in Moses. Yet the conclusion of this first phase of making the Israelites a people belonging to God was to give them His revelation. This was the great moment the Torah was revealed, a day seared into the heart of every Hebrew man and woman.

Now there is another meaning to this great feast, and I wonder if you caught it when you read God's commandments for the Feast of Weeks in Leviticus 23. Here we find the rather surprising commandment that two loaves were to be waved before the Lord, and they were to be made *with* leaven. Are you shocked? After all, leaven is the biblical symbol of sin and wickedness, as we've seen. Why in the world would God want loaves made with leaven to be used in His holy festival?

Don't be troubled. This is the good news for you! These two loaves are symbols of the very reason that you and I are in Christ, in the church of Jesus, and in the Kingdom of God. It is because God has mercy on sinners! These two loaves represent sinful mankind. They represent men with the sinful nature "baked" in them. Yet in the latter part of the harvest of Israel, God wanted Israel to remember the outsiders, and so He commanded that these very loaves be waved before Him in gratitude. Gentiles – those "leavened" ones outside "unleavened" Israel – are going to be welcomed too.

Obviously, God was thinking of the great unwashed majority of humanity, not just the pure Israelites. This is confirmed by that rather out-of-place commandment at the end of all God's instructions for the Feast of Weeks. Here it is:

> "When you reap the harvest of your land, do not reap to the very edges of your field or gather the gleanings of your harvest. . . . Leave them for the poor and the foreigner. I am the LORD your God" (Leviticus 19:9-10, NIV).

God is saying to Israel, *Remember the Gentiles. Remember that you are blessed to be a blessing. Remember that I intend to redeem the whole earth, not just Israel. Don't forget them, rich and poor, in all that you do, even in how you bring in the harvests I give you.*

The great fulfillment of this promise came, of course, on the Day of Pentecost. Remember that Pentecost is the Greek name for the Feast of Weeks. It means "fifty," referring to the fifty days after the Feast of Firstfruits on which the festival occurred. In the waving of two loaves made with leaven and in the command to leave some of the harvest for the poor, God was showing His people that He cared for the wider world outside Israel.

If there was ever a day that fulfilled this divine concern, it was the Day of Pentecost. On that day, the disciples gathered in Jerusalem as Jesus had commanded them to do before He ascended to the Father. According to Acts 1:4-8, they had been commanded not to depart from Jerusalem, but to wait there until they were endued with power from on high to become witnesses unto Him in Jerusalem, Samaria, and the uttermost parts of the earth.

We know from Acts 1:13 that the disciples gathered in an upper room in a house in the city, and there they chose Judas's successor. However, according to Acts 2:1-4 when the Holy Spirit was poured out, He filled them and "the house" where they were assembled. But the tradition of saying the Holy Spirit was poured out "in the upper room" is not supported by the text.

When the Holy Spirit was poured out, He filled them and "the house" where they were assembled.

The Holy Spirit was poured out upon the approximate 120 believers in a house in Jerusalem. We learn from Acts 2 that many were there from Gentile nations: Parthians, Medes, and Elamites; residents of Mesopotamia, Judea, and Cappadocia, Pontus, Asia, Phrygia, Pamphylia, Egypt, and parts of Libya near Cyrene; visitors from Rome (both Jews and converts to Judaism); Cretans and Arabians. More than fifteen Gentile lands are mentioned as looking on, and many of these were born again after Peter preached and explained who Jesus and the Holy Spirit are.

What greater fulfillment of God's passion for the lost Gentile world than for a New Covenant church to arise comprised of every tribe and tongue? What better fulfillment of the twin symbols of harvest and leavened bread but that the Gentiles are harvested for the gospel of Jesus Christ and filled with the Spirit of the living God? How perfectly the Day of Pentecost, as we know it from our New Testament, fulfills the heart of God expressed in the Feast of Weeks – as we know it from our Old Testament.

Thank God for His mercy, as the Apostle Paul wrote, to those of us who were "excluded from citizenship in Israel and foreigners to the covenants of the promise, without hope and without God in the world" (Ephesians 2:12, NIV). Thank God for the meaning and the fulfillment of the Feast of Weeks!

Devouring Fire and Everlasting Burnings

"John answered, saying unto them all, I indeed baptize you with water; but one mightier than I cometh, the latchet of whose shoes I am not worthy to unloose: he shall baptize you with the Holy Ghost and with fire" (Luke 3:16).

"There appeared unto them cloven tongues like as of fire, and it sat upon each of them" (Acts 2:3).

"The sinners in Zion are afraid; fearfulness hath surprised the hypocrites. Who among us shall dwell with the devouring fire? who among us shall dwell with everlasting burnings?" (Isaiah 33:14).

I wish to share with you a prophetic word of warning and encouragement. You have been set on a collision course with your adversary. You were built for that battle and created for that conflict.

Your armor prophesies warfare, and your enemy is about to encounter a God with whom he cannot contend, nor can he fence in nor flee from God's manifest presence.

The God who has heretofore been fighting with you is about to fight for you!

Through recognition of God's Feast of Weeks, we draw a direct line to its historical fulfillment and genesis in the teachings of our Lord regarding the outpouring and infilling of the mighty Holy Spirit that came in Acts 2.

I am inspired by the words of A. W. Tozer, who wrote, "The average Christian is so cold and contented with his wretched condition that there is no vacuum of desire into which the blessed Spirit can rush in satisfying fullness."[18]

---

[18] Tozer, A.W. *Born After Midnight*. Camp Hill, PA: Christian Publications, 1992. Print, p. 7.

I am further inspired by the words of Charles H. Spurgeon: "Apart from the spirit of God we can do nothing. We are ships without the wind or chariots without steeds to pull them; like branches without sap, we are withered."[19]

Here are those pointed words from the original Pentecostal prophet Joel:

> "It shall come to pass afterward, that I will pour out my spirit upon all flesh; and your sons and your daughters shall prophesy, your old men shall dream dreams, your young men shall see visions" (2:28).

The Apostle Peter said the holy angels of God would desire to understand this mystery (1 Peter 1:12). Zechariah said it would fall like rain (Zechariah 10:1), and Amos said it would take some preparation (Amos 4:7). Hosea preached that it would require the breaking up of our fallow ground (Hosea 10:12). But I love the picture that Malachi painted: suddenly He will come to His temple (Malachi 3:1)!

Through the Pentecostal experience, we are promised power to propel us across that great Old and New Covenant theological divide and realize that the God in Christ becomes the Christ in us, and as Jesus put a face on the Father, so now we put a face on Jesus to this dying world.

> "What? know ye not that your body is the temple of the Holy Ghost which is in you, which ye have of God, and ye are not your own?" (1 Corinthians 6:19).

> "We have this treasure in earthen vessels, that the excellency of the power may be of God, and not of us" (2 Corinthians 4:7).

> "There is therefore now no condemnation to them which are in Christ Jesus, who walk not after the flesh, but after the Spirit" (Romans 8:1).

---

[19] Spurgeon, Charles Haddon. *Spurgeon's Sermons Volume 20: 1874*. From sermon delivered on January 4, 1874, "Life More Abundant" (No. 1150).

"Even the Spirit of truth; whom the world cannot receive, because it seeth him not, neither knoweth him: but ye know him; for he dwelleth with you, and shall be in you" (John 14:17).

There is only one reason to have a body, and that is to give expression to the life within it! Many people enjoy shaking my hand. However, if it was severed from my body in an accident, I am certain there would be far less interest.

The Spirit of God within us gives us – as individuals and as the church at large – the connection to the Spirit of God that makes both our natural body and the body of Christ on earth alive with vitality, power, and purpose.

Unfortunately, we live in a time when a powerless Pentecost has become the norm and not the exception. We have more perversion than power, more playboys than prophets, and more compromise than conviction. We need the One who condescends to indwell mortals, to fill us full of Himself. But let us first count the cost.

Though Pentecost meant power to the disciples, it was also prison to them. Pentecost meant enduement, but it also meant banishment from organized religion. Pentecost meant favor with God. It also brought hatred from men. Pentecost brought tremendous miracles. It also brought mighty obstacles.

Why do we have to hang a sign outside our church to announce we are Pentecostal? Because without a sign no one could identify us. Most of the time the sign outside the church is the only sign they will see, for when they get inside they find nothing more than placating pastors who are afraid and ashamed to speak in tongues lest the practice offend someone of influence or their television audience.

Just pass through a town after it has been torn apart by a tornado, and I assure you that you will not have to be told that a mighty wind has cleared the place. In the same way, a fire is self-announcing. Because we don't pray in tongues in private, we have no power in public. Our emptiness of heaven's language makes us

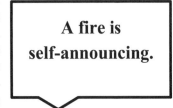

A fire is self-announcing.

void of an earthly word. We have the best of pressed suits, but we don't pierce the spirit with our prayers.

We have a shout in the sanctuary but no clout in the spirit. We claim authority but take no meaningful ground. We write songs of victory over evil that are suitable for the playground, not the battleground. We have become proficient in the dialect of men but empty of the voice of heaven.

Many who claim they have experienced the baptism of the Holy Ghost are more dead than alive, more off than on, more wrong than right. Some are more spirit-frilled than Spirit-filled. We have been used to the outer fringe of His works and have forgotten the inner essence of His power.

Whenever evil mires the work of God, our flesh reasserts itself, and our lack of fruit condemns our prayerless, powerless, passionless Christianity. We need another drenching downpour of Pentecostal power.

On the Day of Pentecost, Peter prayed ten days and preached ten minutes. Now we pray ten minutes and preach ten days. No wonder we have so many failures. Today the Holy Spirit is more ignored than denied.

I think God's people are ready to lose their dignity for a demonstration, their degrees for revelation, their marketing for miracles, their reputation for repentance, and their tongues of poison for tongues of fire.

A prophecy of apostasy as spoken in 1 Timothy 4:1 should never surprise us:

> "Now the Spirit speaketh expressly, that in the latter times some shall depart from the faith, giving heed to seducing spirits, and doctrines of devils."

The apostate church will continue its cold indifference to a true move of God's Holy Spirit in the earth even as the true apostolic church continues to seek divine encounter, grows to maturity, and prepares the earth for the imminent return of our Lord and Savior, Jesus Christ.

Context is important. If you're enjoying a good movie at a theater and shout "Fire!" the authorities will lock you up. However, we need some preachers and believers in this hour to shout "Fire!" – Holy Ghost fire – in church to see multitudes saved, healed, and delivered.

Here in Isaiah 33, we have the ancient prophet's riveting pronouncement to Jerusalem and Judah regarding their invasion by and deliverance from the Assyrian army under Sennacherib. From the lines in verse 14, we have illuminated by the Holy Spirit a great revelation of God as Father by discovering two distinct properties of fire: "Who among us shall dwell with [abide in] the devouring fire?"

God Almighty desires to permanently remove from your life anything you don't want and everything you don't need by your surrendering them to Him and exposing them to the white hot heat of the Holy Spirit.

This is the "devouring fire" of the presence of God available to you and me. Oh, that His glory would annihilate everything in our lives that would hinder His full blessing from resting upon us. May we all plead to burn it out: "O blessed Holy Spirit, make me by Your fire pure and clean." And in the words of Zechariah 14:20, "Holiness unto the LORD."

The second property of fire is to amalgamate, to join two as one in a permanent state. "Who among us shall dwell with [abide in] 'everlasting burnings?'" (Isaiah 33:14). Here is the fulfillment of the High Priestly prayer of our Lord in John 17:21, "That they all may be one; as thou, Father, art in me, and I in thee, that they also may be one in us: that the world may believe that thou hast sent me." Our prayer must become that we are so melted by the baptism of Pentecostal fire that those areas of inconsistence and fluctuation in our devotion to

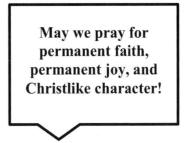

May we pray for permanent faith, permanent joy, and Christlike character!

Christ and our influence upon this generation are fused into the steadfast consistency of His Spirit. May we pray for permanent faith, permanent joy, permanent peace, abiding commitment, and Christ-like character!

A final thought regarding fire. These scriptures set the tone:

"The light of Israel shall be for a fire, and his Holy One for a flame" (Isaiah 10:17).

"Our God is a consuming fire" (Hebrews 12:29).

"Then I beheld, and lo a likeness as the appearance of fire: from the appearance of his loins even downward, fire; and from his loins even upward, as the appearance of brightness, as the colour of amber" (Ezekiel 8:2).

"His eyes were as a flame of fire" (Revelation 19:12).

Once again, Luke 3:16 promises that the Lord Jesus Christ will baptize us in fire. I believe this teaches us that we can become totally immersed in God so that we become peace, joy, hope, healing, and so on. In other words, we die in the fiery ocean of His presence and resurrect in the permanence and consistency of His character. Oh, may His presence and the power of Pentecost seal you today.

WISDOM OF THE RABBIS

Happy are the people who learn from the Shofar! Shofar wakes, calls the alarm, announces royalty, trumpets victory, signals God's power – and mercy. Shofar recalls the ram whose hidden presence in the bushes saved our beloved father, Isaac. ~ *Makom Ohr Shalom Machzor*

On Yom Kippur, we stand before God, hand on heart and say, "God: it's not your fault." We take responsibility. We are not who we should be, so life is not what it could be. We are the problem in the relationship, not You.

~ *Rabbi Shaul Rosenblatt*

Yom Kippur is not about personal resolutions and private reflection. It is about standing up and talking to God. It is about apologizing, about reestablishing our connection with our Creator. We must tell God who we are, where we are holding in life, and what we know needs improvement.

~ *Rabbi Dovid Rosenfeld*

On Rosh Hashanah, everything we do is imbued with extreme significance. We stand in judgment before the Heavenly Court while each of our actions, words, and thoughts are scrutinized.

~ *Rabbi Moshe Schuchman*

The sukkah, the booth, is the central symbol of the ancient Israelites' trust and hope for forty years in the desert. The Hebrews left the protection of man-made thick walls to place themselves under the protection of God. Exposed to dangerous natural conditions and hostile roving bands, they placed their confidence in the divine concern, which is the only true source of security. ~ *Rabbi Irving Greenberg*

Chapter VI

THE FEASTS OF GOD:
THE FALL FESTIVALS

The fall festivals start in Tishrei in the Hebrew calendar, which is September in our Gregorian calendars. This is quite a jump in time from the Feast of Pentecost! Remember with me that the first three feasts of God occurred in the first month of the Hebrew calendar, Nisan, which is approximately April. Pentecost occurs in late May or early June.

The Feast of Trumpets, the first of the fall festivals, occurs on the first of Tishrei. This vast leap in time parallels a vast leap in the emphases of the feasts.

The spring feasts of God were about redemption, deliverance, God's abundant provision, and the revelation of God given to the Jews but meant for all nations on earth. The Fall Feasts are heavier in tone. They are about awakening, repentance, God's judgment, and ultimately God making all things new.

There is another great difference between the spring festivals and the fall festivals of God. The spring festivals are entirely fulfilled in the life of Jesus Christ and in the coming of the Holy Spirit on the Day of Pentecost. However, most Christian teachers believe that the fall festivals are yet unfulfilled; they are prophetic statements awaiting the second coming of our Lord. This makes them both thrilling and challenging, both exciting and sometimes difficult to interpret.

The Feast of Trumpets

The first of these celebrations is the Festival of Trumpets, which in Hebrew is *Yom Teruah* (yahm tuh-RU-AH), meaning "day of noise." The more common name for this feast among Jews is *Rosh Hashanah*, which literally means "head of the year."

DIVINE ENCOUNTER

During this time which includes Ten Days of Awe and concludes on Yom Kippur, the Day of Atonement, there is a divine activity that is quite unusual and remarkable. The period is marked by God with a reversal of roles, if you will, which I liken to a type of divine withdrawal or a Rosh Hashanah retreat.

Through His Word, God Almighty gives us less direction and information of this period of the year than any of the other feast periods. It feels almost like a "baiting" of sorts by our Father, a time where He is saying to us, "If you want to know…seek…Me!" As the Psalmist says in Psalm 27:8, "When thou saidst, Seek ye my face; my heart said unto thee, Thy face, LORD, will I seek."

At this very special time of year, our Father wants us to be keenly aware that the prerogative is His. We cannot even seek Him unless He gives us that desire and when He does, then the responsibility shifts to us to "seek" His face.

This is a period where God, in a way, withdraws His presence to see if it creates a hunger and thirst for His presence sufficient to cause us to abandon all else in pursuit of Him.

The song, "Clear the Stage©[20]," beautifully captures what I'm speaking of in its powerful and prophetic lyrics. They remind us to clear the stage of our lives by crushing our idols, seeking repentance and God's presence in unadulterated praise and worship to Him and Him alone.

ᵍ   ᵍ   ᵍ

"The LORD said to Moses, 'Say to the Israelites, 'On the first day of the seventh month you are to have a day of Sabbath rest, a sacred assembly commemorated with trumpet blasts. Do no regular work but present a food offering to the LORD'" (Leviticus 23:23-25, NIV).

"On the first day of the seventh month, hold a sacred assembly and do no regular work. It is a day for you to sound the trumpets. As an aroma pleasing to the LORD, offer a burnt

---

[20] 2002 Ross King Music.

offering of one young bull, one ram and seven male lambs a year old, all without defect" (Numbers 29:1-2, NIV).

Again, God's directives regarding this period encompassing Rosh Hashanah (Trumpets), Ten Days of Awe, and Yom Kippur (Day of Atonement) are unusually limited. It begins on the first day of the seventh month. It is a day of sabbath rest with an assembly and no labor. It has a commanded offering. It is to be a day of the Sounding of the Trumpet (shofar).

It could be that our Father is saying much by saying little. By so doing, could it be that He is again placing the responsibility on us? As if to say this one is on you and will be all that you choose to make it? I think so. While there is little in scripture regarding Rosh Hashanah, we do have wonderful insight provided to us by the sages and in the Talmud.

These historic writings reveal a bit more about this very sacred period which was communicated to Moses from Jehovah and passed down orally from generation to generation. Rosh Hashanah is celebrated by the Jewish people not only as the Head of the Year but also as the anniversary of God creating the world and mankind. And our Creator, at this time, examines or judges the universe, the world of men, and individuals.

On Rosh Hashanah, God opens the book. Now don't allow this book of account to be a point of confusion for you. Some teach that this book is the same as the Lamb's book of life found in the book of Revelation, but that's not the case.

It's only appropriate to teach on the book of life once Jesus established the New Covenant. When Jesus made propitiation at Calvary, we entered into the New Covenant with eternal life secured through the blood of our spotless Lamb and our names are recorded in His book of life.

Here, we're studying the Old Covenant practice where the book of account records the righteous or wicked actions of man for one year. So the book is opened and for ten days, God judges from it, then closes or seals it on Yom Kippur for another year thus sealing the fate of the next year. It is to be a time of deep introspection and repentance.

Remember the first message of John the Baptist was "repent" as was the first message of Jesus Christ. According to the sages, it is also a day for the coronation of our God as King, both on a personal level and national level as the absolute sovereign of the world and all that in it is. The Talmud records words to the effect of God asking for us to "talk to Him and say before Him that your remembrance comes before Him for good." Meaning, you make Me your sovereign, your King by declaring it before Me on this day.

> **The first message of John the Baptist was "repent" as was the first message of Jesus Christ.**

In regard to this act of declared sovereignty, keep in mind Psalm 2:7, "I will declare the decree: The LORD has said to Me, 'You are My Son, Today I have begotten You.'" and also Proverbs 18:21, "Death and life are in the power of the tongue."

Unlike all other feasts, Rosh Hashanah and Yom Kippur were not established to commemorate significant events in Israel's national history. We know that the Feast of Passover celebrates the deliverance of God's people from slavery in Egypt. The Feast of Unleavened Bread commemorates the fact that when the Israelites were finally freed from bondage in Egypt, they had to flee so quickly that there was no time to let their bread rise.

The Feast of Firstfruits was established in Leviticus 23:10, "...When ye be come into the land which I give unto you, and shall reap the harvest thereof, then ye shall bring a sheaf of the firstfruits of your harvest unto the priest:" The Feast of Pentecost is based on the Israelite tradition that Moses received the Law on Mount Sinai exactly fifty days after Firstfruits. And of course, the Feast of Tabernacles commemorates the forty year period following their freedom from bondage when the Israelites lived in temporary shelters during their wilderness experience.

During this feast, the Israelites were required to leave the comfort of their homes and live in tabernacles or booths – three sided temporary structures with leafy roofs through which the stars could be seen. In this way they would remember how their ancestors had lived in booths or tents when they came out of slavery in Egypt.

Rosh Hashanah and Yom Kippur are not historic in application but speak to us of immediacy, the there and the now of divine encounter!

According to the Genesis record, our separation from God was due to His withdrawal from us as a direct result of sin. So our Father withdraws during this time as we become acutely aware of our desire for and need of His presence and realize that still sin separates. Thanks be to God, Genesis 3 also records the prophecy of our propitiation! Jesus Christ and His precious blood cleanses us from all unrighteousness, Romans 5:19, "For as by one man's disobedience many were made sinners, so by the obedience of one shall many be made righteous."

During this period of Rosh Hashanah retreat, I'm always mindful of the Lord Jesus and the disciples in Mark 4:35-39:

"And the same day, when the even was come, he saith unto them, Let us pass over unto the other side. And when they had sent away the multitude, they took him even as he was in the ship. And there were also with him other little ships.

"And there arose a great storm of wind, and the waves beat into the ship, so that it was now full. And he was in the hinder part of the ship, asleep on a pillow: and they awake him, and say unto him, Master, carest thou not that we perish?

"And he arose, and rebuked the wind, and said unto the sea, Peace, be still. And the wind ceased, and there was a great calm."

Here Jesus is withdrawn, at rest, asleep, in fact. When one sleeps, they are not "gone or dead." They simply are not manifesting their presence outwardly or externally. However, His repose caused His followers to seek Him, find Him, and awaken Him!

This is a major lesson of Rosh Hashanah, that He is not dead. For if He were not alive for even one millisecond, all the universe would crumble and cease to exist! Colossians 1:17, "He is before all things, and in him all things hold together."

He's alive and His divine intent is encounter. This time He does not leave the ninety-nine and seek us, but rather He creates a vacuum of His presence to stimulate our pursuit of Him. He desperately wants us to awaken Him, declare His kingship, and crown Him our Sovereign, the undisputed Lord of this world and every kingdom of our lives.

To the Jewish mind, crowning God as the sovereign King is much different than it is to our understanding. It is a relationship created by subjects, not as a result of an overpowering, demanding, forced "lording over" by the King or His law!

Our blessed Lord retreats and says, "I will not force you. If you crown Me king, it is only because by the power of My cross I purchased your right of choice to do so completely of your own volition!" There is no demanding dictator here. Deuteronomy 30:19:

"I call heaven and earth to record this day against you, that I have set before you life and death, blessing and cursing: therefore choose life, that both thou and thy seed may live:"

In Psalm 27:8 when God says to us "seek My face," He creates a vacuum of His presence and waits for us to declare of our own will a resounding "thy face, Lord, will I seek!"

Psalm 42:1 echoes, "As the hart (deer) panteth after the water brooks, so panteth my soul after thee, O God." 2 Chronicles 15:2 promises, "...If you seek Him, He will be found of you..."

Under the Old Covenant in Psalms, David said, "Lord, examine me," but under the New Covenant, Paul, in 1 Corinthians 11:28 says, "examine yourself."

Especially during Rosh Hashanah and the Days of Awe, which for New Testament believers can be celebrated every day, may we examine ourselves and eat that bread and drink that cup. May we, in humility and with a repentant heart, seek Him, find Him, and crown Him king. What a divine encounter will await us as we do!

Now let's discuss the main word that comprises the name of this feast – trumpets!

God seems to like the sound of trumpets. Some have suggested that God has loved the biblical ram's horn trumpet, called the *shofar* (show-FAHR), since Isaac was spared by a ram caught in a thicket by its horn.

Those who believe this argue that without Isaac, we would not have the Jews and without the Jews we would not have the Messiah, the Bible, the apostles, or all that follows after. Perhaps this truth is the source of God's love for the shofar.

Although other kinds of trumpets are mentioned in the Bible – silver trumpets, for example, were used in Israel for signaling camp movements, for carrying out Temple rituals, and for calling troops to battle – the shofar is certainly God's favorite. It is mentioned in the Bible more than any other musical instrument. The blowing of a shofar summoned Israel to meet with God (Exodus 19:13). It proclaimed the Year of Jubilee (Leviticus 25:8-10). It both summoned God's people to repentance (Joel 2:15) and warned of trouble (Joel 2:1). Yet most impressive of all, the shofar was blown more than one hundred times on Rosh Hashanah, the Feast of Trumpets.

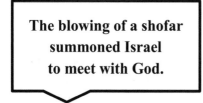

The blowing of a shofar summoned Israel to meet with God.

The blowing of a ram's horn is so important in the life of Israel that four standard blasts are traditionally used. The first is the *Tekiah* (te-KEE-ah), which is a long single blast. The *Sheviah* (sh-EV-ee-ah) are three short blasts that sound like a human wail and call God's people to repentance. The *Te-ruah* (tuh-RU-AH), comprised of nine blasts intended to sound like an alarm, calls the faithful to repentance. *Tekiah ha'Gadol* (te-KEE-ah ha-guh-dol) is a great blast that lasts as long as the *baal tekiah* (buh-ahl te-KEE-ah) – the shofar virtuoso – has breath to sustain it.

So, on the day of this great feast, there was a sacred assembly. The trumpet was blown repeatedly as a call to remembrance and as a summons to repentance. The main purpose was to send the all-important signal, "Awake!" Food was offered to the Lord as a sacrifice, and the people ate together as well. In more modern times, Jewish people also light candles, eat apples dipped in honey, enjoy *challah* (KHAH-luh) shaped like a crown, and literally and symbolically begin a thorough process of repentance.

Prophetic insights indicate that the second coming of Jesus could very well occur on Rosh Hashanah! Of course, nobody knows exactly when Jesus is coming back. It might be years from this moment, or it might be before you turn this page. Let me explain. Listen to what the Apostle Paul wrote about the second coming of Jesus:

> "The Lord himself will come down from heaven, with a loud command, with the voice of the archangel and with the trumpet call of God, and the dead in Christ will rise first. After that, we who are still alive and are left will be caught up together with them in the clouds to meet the Lord in the air. And so we will be with the Lord forever" (1 Thessalonians 4:16-17, NIV).

> "Listen, I tell you a mystery: We will not all sleep, but we will all be changed – in a flash, in the twinkling of an eye, at the last trumpet. For the trumpet will sound, the dead will be raised imperishable, and we will be changed. For the perishable must clothe itself with the imperishable, and the mortal with immortality" (1 Corinthians 15:51-53, NIV).

You see how clear this is? The last trumpet will sound, and we will rise to be with Jesus. I know that God could make a trumpet sound anytime He chooses. Yet it seems to me that our God who is so careful about types and shadows, who plans out prophecy and fulfillment, types and metaphors, in such grand detail, and who established a Feast of Trumpets on which the shofar is blown one hundred times would return on the very day when a trumpet will be the signal of His coming. It's certainly possible that Jesus will make His return on the day that for millennia has been called the Feast of Trumpets!

Days of Awe

Just as with many of God's feasts, there is a special purpose for the time between the Feast of Trumpets and the next feast, *Yom Kippur* or the "Day of Atonement." These ten days are called the "Days of Awe," or *Yamim Noraim* in Hebrew (YAH-meem NOH reh-eem), which means "Days of Repentance."

Jewish tradition teaches that at Rosh Hashanah, God sits on His throne of judgment and evaluates His creation. Each of us is on trial and judged. God writes the names of both the extremely righteous and the extremely wicked in the appropriate books on Rosh Hashanah. Most people, though, are a mixture of good and evil, so they can alter how God sees them with what they do during the ten days between Rosh Hashanah and Yom Kippur (the Day of Atonement), which is the holiest day of all. During this time, the people of God repent of their sins, reconcile with others, seek God in prayer, and do good deeds.

The posture of our hearts during these ten Days of Awe mirror the shape of the shofar used to usher in this period of reflection. The shofar is bent; its head pointed to the ground. The ram's horn shofar is not made by man; it is made by God and designed with this bent shape. During this period, God withdraws from us to ensure that we look at ourselves and earnestly seek His face.

Bowing before the King of the Universe in our repentant posture, we invite God to be crowned as King of every area of our hearts and lives. We invite Him to be King over the mundane details – the intricacies of our lives – and we invoke the coronation of His kingship afresh.

We should learn from the message of these ten days. Though repentance is our calling every day of the year and though we should be quick to seek God for forgiveness of our sins, there is also a special need in our lives to be pure. A special level of repentance and cleansing ourselves should occur when we know we are about to stand before God, when we know that it is Him "with whom we have to do" (Hebrews 4:13).

I'm certainly grateful that the author of Hebrews also wrote, "Let us then approach God's throne of grace with confidence, so that we may receive mercy and find grace to help us in our time of need" (Hebrews 4:16, NIV). I'm grateful for the access to God that we have through the blood of Jesus. Yet I am always aware that the author of Hebrews also said, "It is a dreadful thing to fall into the hands of the living God" (Hebrews 10:31, NIV). The Days of Awe remind me that

I want to be pure and holy before my God. I want to be part of that Bride of Christ who has "made herself ready" for the "wedding of the Lamb" (Revelation 19:7, NIV).

Day of Atonement

The highest and holiest day in the Hebrew calendar is the Day of Atonement, or *Yom Kippur*. It is the sixth of the major feasts of God and takes place on the tenth day of the seventh month. On this day and on this day only, the high priest of God was permitted to enter the Holy of Holies of the Temple and make atonement for the sins of God's people. It was a somber day of fasting and humility as well as deep repentance for the sins of the year.

> "The LORD said to Moses, 'The tenth day of this seventh month is the Day of Atonement. Hold a sacred assembly and deny yourselves, and present a food offering to the LORD. Do not do any work on that day, because it is the Day of Atonement, when atonement is made for you before the LORD your God. Those who do not deny themselves on that day must be cut off from their people. I will destroy from among their people anyone who does any work on that day. You shall do no work at all. This is to be a lasting ordinance for the generations to come, wherever you live. It is a day of sabbath rest for you, and you must deny yourselves. From the evening of the ninth day of the month until the following evening you are to observe your sabbath" (Leviticus 23:26-32, NIV).

To understand the power of this day, we should remember God's words to Moses after the deaths of Aaron's sons, Nadab and Abihu. In Leviticus 10, Nadab and Abihu went about their priestly duties in an unauthorized way. The Bible tells us that fire came out from the presence of the Lord and killed the two men. In Leviticus 16:2, God spoke to Moses about the incident and said:

> "Tell your brother Aaron that he is not to come whenever he chooses into the Most Holy Place behind the curtain in front of the atonement cover on the ark, or else he will die. For I will appear in the cloud over the atonement cover" (NIV).

What follows in Leviticus 16 is precisely how Aaron is to enter the Holy of Holies and make atonement for the people.

God is a King, and His subjects are not to approach Him without invitation during this time, without knowing how the King chooses for His people to draw near. This truth hovers over the Day of Atonement. The Lord God is King of the universe and will be approached only on His own terms and by His own decree. What we know of our God is that He desires purity, holiness, and humility. He calls for these things on this Day of Atonement above all days.

Consider for a moment the intricate requirements God placed upon the high priest of Israel for entering the Holy of Holies on the Day of Atonement. The priest had to wash himself completely and put on the pure linen garments that were specifically designed to keep all flesh from view. He also donned the rest of his priestly garments. He then stood before the Lord, confessing his sins and the sins of his house as a bull was brought before the Lord.

The bull was killed and its blood put into a basin. Two goats were then brought before the Lord. These were given by the congregation. By the casting of lots, one of these goats was chosen as a sacrifice and the other as the "scapegoat." The high priest then took coals from the brazen altar, put them in a censer, added incense, and proceeded behind the veil of the tabernacle. The smoke of the censer filled the Holy of Holies.

Next the high priest came out of the tabernacle, retrieved the basin of bull's blood, and returned to the tabernacle beyond the veil. There he sprinkled the bull's blood on the Ark of the Covenant and then left the tabernacle again. Outside, he killed the goat chosen for sacrifice before the Lord and took its blood back into the tabernacle to sprinkle the Ark. Finally, the priest went outside and laid his hands on the remaining goat, confessed the sins of Israel over it, and sent the goat away into an uninhabited land.

These steps were required because the King of all the universe wished to be approached in this manner. He wanted purity. He wanted no flesh involved. He wanted the shedding of blood. He wanted sin removed. He wanted all done in holy fear and reverence. This was the meaning of the Day of Atonement.

Consider for a moment that had nothing changed, we would still be a people awaiting access to the presence of God on one day a year. We would still be hoping for acceptance by the King of the universe based on our deeds. We would still be utterly dependent upon a high priest atoning for us with the blood of bulls and goats.

This would be our sorry state if Jesus had not come, if He had not become our once and for all High Priest before God. But thank God, He did!

Listen to the glorious words from the book of Hebrews that tell us Jesus did once and for all what all the high priests of history never could have done:

> "When Christ came as high priest of the good things that are now already here, he went through the greater and more perfect tabernacle that is not made with human hands, that is to say, is not a part of this creation. He did not enter by means of the blood of goats and calves; but he entered the Most Holy Place once for all by his own blood, thus obtaining eternal redemption.

> "The blood of goats and bulls and the ashes of a heifer sprinkled on those who are ceremonially unclean sanctify them so that they are outwardly clean. How much more, then, will the blood of Christ, who through the eternal Spirit offered himself unblemished to God, cleanse our consciences from acts that lead to death, so that we may serve the living God!

> "For this reason Christ is the mediator of a new covenant, that those who are called may receive the promised eternal inheritance – now that he has died as a ransom to set them free from the sins committed under the first covenant" (Hebrews 9:11-15, NIV).

> "When this priest had offered for all time one sacrifice for sins, he sat down at the right hand of God, and since that time he waits for his enemies to be made his footstool. For by one sacrifice he has made perfect forever those who are being made holy" (Hebrews 10:12-14, NIV).

> "Brothers and sisters, since we have confidence to enter the Most Holy Place by the blood of Jesus, by a new and living

way opened for us through the curtain, that is, his body, and since we have a great priest over the house of God, let us draw near to God with a sincere heart and with the full assurance that faith brings, having our hearts sprinkled to cleanse us from a guilty conscience and having our bodies washed with pure water" (Hebrews 10:19-23, NIV).

This is now the meaning of the Day of Atonement for a New Covenant people. We no longer must rely on the blood of bulls and goats. We no longer must rely on the purity of a high priest who once a year has trembling access to the Holy of Holies. Now, because of what Jesus, our great High Priest, has done, we can now "come boldly unto the throne of grace, that we may obtain mercy, and find grace to help in time of need" (Hebrews 4:16). For us, the Day of Atonement has become an atoned-for life that never ends.

As I mentioned previously in The Red Blood Moons chapter, it's during this Fall feast season that our adversary wages warfare and unleashes chaos into every arena imaginable. From the atrocious autumn tragedy of September 11, 2011 to numerous other terror attacks and senseless acts of violence even as recently as the fall of 2014, to the stock market plunging in several different years during this time, it is evident that the enemy launches all out attacks during this season. Not only that, history proves that many wars have started during this time, and numerous earthquakes, hurricanes, and volcano eruptions have occurred in the fall of the year.

Perhaps it's because our enemy knows that the Feasts of Passover and Pentecost have been fulfilled but not the Feast of Tabernacles and this could very well be the time that the Lord returns for His church. And if He doesn't, Joel 2 bears out that we will receive a double portion! That's why he bombards with such vicious onslaughts during this particular season.

So understanding the backdrop surrounding the Tabernacles season and Day of Atonement certainly puts these passages from Joel 2 in a completely new light and promises these seven anointings of the Atonement:

1. "Be glad then, ye children of Zion, and rejoice in the LORD your God: for he hath given you the former rain moderately, and he will cause to come down for you the

rain, the former rain, and the latter rain in the first month." You'll receive a double portion from the Lord, the former and the latter rain" (Joel 2:23).

2. "And the floors shall be full of wheat, and the fats shall overflow with wine and oil." You'll receive a financial breakthrough in your life" (Joel 2:24).

3. "And I will restore to you the years that the locust hath eaten, the cankerworm, and the caterpiller, and the palmerworm, my great army which I sent among you." The devil will be forced to restore the years the locusts have eaten, and nothing you've lost is going to stay lost!" (Joel 2:25).

4. "...the LORD your God, that hath dealt wondrously with you: ..." Either Jesus will return in the rapture or miracles will begin exploding in your life!" (Joel 2:26).

5. "And ye shall know that I am in the midst of Israel..." The divine presence of Jesus Himself will be in your midst" (Joel 2:27).

6. "And it shall come to pass afterward, that I will pour out my spirit upon all flesh; and your sons and your daughters shall prophesy, your old men shall dream dreams, your young men shall see visions:" There's going to be an increase of revelation knowledge poured into your life and that of your family's lives" (Joel 2:28).

7. "And it shall come to pass, that whosoever shall call on the name of the LORD shall be delivered:" Deliverance is promised to you, and nothing can stop you or block you when God sets you free!: (Joel 2:32).

Thank God for His abundant blessings in our lives and powerful promises in His Word as we rejoice in the continued revelation of His feast seasons!

The Feast of Tabernacles

It may be observed that the season of Tabernacles can be divided into two distinct portions. The first consists of the period of time compromising of Rosh Hashanah, Yom Kippur, and the Days of

Awe. And the second being that of the Feast of Tabernacles itself. The first being a time of examination and the second a time of celebration and intimacy. This period includes *Simchah, Increasing Simchah*, concluding in *Simchat Torah* which is a Jewish holiday that occurs at the end of the Feast of Tabernacles. As the celebration comes to a conclusion, the Jewish people begin the reading cycle of the Torah.

The seventh and final festival of God, the Feast of Tabernacles, occurred on the fifteenth day of the seventh month, which would always be the seventh full moon of the year. The Hebrew name for this feast is *Sukkot* (soo-KOTE), which means "booths." More than anything else, this feast is about the people of God recalling God's provision of shelter when they first came out of Egypt.

"The LORD said to Moses, 'Say to the Israelites: 'On the fifteenth day of the seventh month the LORD's Festival of Tabernacles begins, and it lasts for seven days. . . . On the first day you are to take branches from luxuriant trees – from palms, willows and other leafy trees – and rejoice before the LORD your God for seven days.

"'Celebrate this as a festival to the LORD . . . each year. . . . Live in temporary shelters for seven days: All native-born Israelites are to live in such shelters so your descendants will know that I had the Israelites live in temporary shelters when I brought them out of Egypt. I am the LORD your God'" (Leviticus 23:33-43, NIV).

This feast is a great occasion of remembrance and of gratitude. Observant Jews today build temporary shelters on rooftops and in backyards, even on balconies. These are called "sukkah." The Jewish sages teach that each sukkah or booth can only reach twenty cubits in height, but there is no limit to their length or width.

This is symbolic of unity and that Sukkot is a time for everyone to be invited and encounter the love of God. It is a time to celebrate with others and to share in the teachings and sayings of the patriarchs. The booth must have at least three sides and must be large enough to house the entire family as well as guests, for the Feast of Tabernacles is very much about inviting outsiders to celebrate the goodness of God, as we will describe in greater detail later.

The Divine Encounter

My lovely wife, Joni, is the perfect balance to my personality. She is rarely emotional or outwardly expressive...or loud.

However, on one occasion she changed my paradigm by weeping. But it wasn't necessarily the tears that changed my revelation of God and my relationship with Him but rather where those tears were falling. They were not dripping from her precious chin onto an altar, we weren't in our prayer meeting, nor receiving Holy Communion. We weren't even in church, nor in the presence of others. In fact, she didn't even know that I was observing her.

No, those tears were splashing in into dish water at our kitchen sink. When I inquired, she simply said, "I just realized that as I fulfill my calling as a wife and mother, God receives it as worship. He has visited me here in the everydayness of my life, and I am overwhelmed by His love and presence."

"I beseech you therefore, brethren, by the mercies of God, that ye present your bodies a living sacrifice, holy, acceptable unto God, which is your reasonable service. And be not conformed to this world: but be ye transformed by the renewing of your mind, that ye may prove what is that good, and acceptable, and perfect, will of God" (Romans 12:1-2).

I'm quite partial to the descriptiveness of The Message Bible to our generation. It reads as follows:

"So here's what I want you to do, God helping you: Take your everyday, ordinary life – your sleeping, eating, going-to-work, and walking-around life – and place it before God as an offering. Embracing what God does for you is the best thing you can do for him. Don't become so well-adjusted to your culture that you fit into it without even thinking. Instead, fix your attention on God. You'll be changed from the inside out."

Notice what God said here: "So here's what I want [not command] YOU to do." God wants us to understand that the responsibility is ours, however, He is "helping you." Here we see that it will require His help which He graciously will provide.

Further what is to be offered, "your body," in the King James Version, not your spirit in this instance. This may seem a stark contrast to my other passages. Not contrary but simply different. God, I believe is here speaking to us that He desires "all of us," which I interpret as much of the deep and glorious revelation of Sukkot.

Take our bodies, or our earthliness ("your sleeping, eating, going-to-work, and walking-around life") and place it before God as an "offering" or, as the King James Version witnesses, "a living sacrifice."

I like that a lot. "Living" to me denotes vibrancy, vitality, energy, motion! I often say that I want to live out loud! Our Father desires for us to thrive in this earth not simply survive in it.

There has been a divorce in the church where we separate the perceived spiritual aspects of our relationship with the Living Christ from perceived natural aspects of that relationship. I've got good news for you: through the revelation of Sukkot, God says to you that He wants to become involved in your "everydayness!"

Through Sukkot, He says I want to be with you when you brush your teeth, drive the kids to school, sit through a sales meeting, write that term paper, make your bed, wash your dishes, mow your lawn, or go to dinner with friends… "your eating, sleeping, going-to-work, walking-around life!"

Think of it this way: He wants to move in with you. He desires no temporary living arrangements, no visit, no hotel room, or vacation into your life. Sukkot declares He wants a permanent home with you!

When you consider it, that's what the elegant garden of Eden was all about – God looking for a home and someone with whom He could live.

Home is a place of comfort and consolation, a place of relaxation and repose, where you (and God) can just be yourself . . . your real self. No pretenses, no masks, no filters. Just the joy of being with those who know you and accept you and love you as you are. Home is the most basic of necessities – shelter. Psalm 61:3, "For thou hast been a shelter for me, and a strong tower from the enemy." What a thought! To be at home, in the everydayness of our earthly journey with our God.

Recently, I had the opportunity to go back home – not to the place of my birth nor of my present residence, but rather to the place of my ancestry. Home for me is Appalachia – the streams and hollows, the deep dark hills of eastern Kentucky.

Whether it's the mountains ablaze with autumn's majesty or a humble home perched on a hillside – these are the *sights* of home. Whether it's the fragrance of a freshly mown field, or fatback frying in a black iron skillet – these are the *smells* of home. Whether it's the hometown harmony of a Gospel quartet, or a coal truck in low gear laboring up the mountainside – these are the *sounds* of home.

Popular culture has capitalized on this instinctive impulse. this divine drive, to get back home.

Do you remember Dorothy and her little dog, Toto, in the Wizard of Oz? They were transported by a tornado to a land beyond time – the magical Land of Oz, where they witnessed wonders, passed through perils, and encountered companions who propelled them toward their primary purpose. They simply wanted to get back home.

And when Dorothy awakened, her wish had come true – she saw her family, friends, and the familiar surroundings of home. It was then that she uttered these words that are indelibly etched on the consciousness of an entire generation: "There's no place like home."

Truer words have never been spoken because whether it's a plush penthouse, a tattered tent, a millionaire's mansion or a country cabin, "There's no place like home."

Home – where your family welcomes you.

Home – where your friends remember you.

Home – where there is provision for every need.

Home – where there is protection from every attack.

Home – where there is healing for every hurt.

Home – where you can feel like you're somebody when you know you ain't nobody.

The Lord Jesus drew reference to God the Father's desired permanent living arrangements with us in John 17:21, "That they all may be one; as thou, Father, art in me, and I in thee, that they also may be one in us: that the world may believe that thou hast sent me."

Solomon described the divine encounter beautifully in Song of Solomon 2:6, "His left hand is under my head, and his right hand doth embrace me." The parallel drawn is this: left representing judgment, keeping at a distance while the right illustrates love, acceptance, and drawing to.

Rosh Hashanah, Yom Kippur, and Days of Awe demonstrate the left hand of God placed upon our head which symbolizes the highest part of our encounter, that relationship between God and our human spirit. But with His right arm He embraces us. Placing His arm around our back as if to say, "I want all of your life, even your back which cannot express your love or devotion back to Me."

God says, "I refuse to let any part of your life go." Not any portions of life which are seen as and are so very spiritual, those face to face encounters of examination but also those joyful and relaxed areas of our daily lives that are the more external and seemingly unrelated to our spirituality – even those our loving Father refuses to let go and squeezes close to Himself in a breathtaking embrace. In short, He wants all of us. Let us determine to hold nothing back. The love of God reaches even to the "back part" of our lives, even to the most insignificant and even mundane moments of our earthly existence.

Yes, His love reaches even there. As Brennan Manning said and I quoted in *The Cross: One Man...One Tree...One Friday*, "I (God) will meet you where you live, and I'll love you as you are, not as you should be ... because you're never going to be as you should be."[21]

This is the unfailing and unfaltering love of our Father expressed through His gift – the supreme gift and sacrifice – the gift of His only begotten Son, nailed by tempered spikes through tortured skin

---

[21] Parsley, Rod. *The Cross: One Man...One Tree...One Friday*. Lake Mary, FL: Charisma House, 2013. Print, pp. 29-30 (*"Brennan Manning on God's Love."* YouTube video recording.)

into splintered wood. Nailed there with welcoming arms out-stretched announcing, "Do I love you? Yes! Yes! A billion times yes! I love you yesterday, and today and forever – through every storm and tempest, every struggle and temptation, from heaven to earth, to hell and back to earth and to heaven again. I love you in life and living, in death and dying, I love you. How much? (*Stretch out your arms*). This much and more. I will not leave you here without Me, nor will I remain in heaven without you. I will bring us together again and we will never be separated, for I am your Father and you are forever My child!"

Leviticus 23:42, "Ye shall dwell in booths seven days; all that are Israelites born shall dwell in booths:" For the seven days of Sukkot, the Jewish people symbolically dwell in their sukkah encountering the Holy One of Israel.

Again, according to Leviticus 23:39-43, the booths were to be used so that Israel would remember the temporary dwellings that were their accommodations during the treacherous track through the wilderness from Egypt to the Promised Land.

Mankind once enjoyed an intimate relationship of divine encounter in the garden of Eden (Genesis 2). Our pristine parents, Adam and Eve, estranged themselves and thereby, the entire human race from this relationship by their sin. Ever since that moment when sin entered the bloodstream of humanity and a chasm was created between Creator and creation, God sought a way to once again dwell, tabernacle, live at home in the midst of His people.

The temporary dwellings Israel built during Tabernacles were reminiscent of a time when God Himself dwelt in the midst of Israel as they made their way through the wilderness. In Exodus 33:14, God told Moses, "...My presence shall go with thee, and I will give thee rest."

We know that God's presence remained in the Tabernacle during their wilderness wanderings, according to Exodus 40:34-38:

> "Then a cloud covered the tent of the congregation, and the glory of the LORD filled the tabernacle. And Moses was not able to enter into the tent of the congregation, because the cloud abode thereon, and the glory of the LORD filled the

tabernacle. And when the cloud was taken up from over the tabernacle, the children of Israel went onward in all their journeys: But if the cloud were not taken up, then they journeyed not till the day that it was taken up. For the cloud of the LORD was upon the tabernacle by day, and fire was on it by night, in the sight of all the house of Israel, throughout all their journeys."

After Israel came into the Promised Land and the Temple was built, God's presence remained there, according to 2 Chronicles 5:13-14:

"It came even to pass, as the trumpeters and singers were as one, to make one sound to be heard in praising and thanking the LORD; and when they lifted up their voice with the trumpets and cymbals and instruments of musick, and praised the LORD, saying, For he is good; for his mercy endureth for ever: that then the house was filled with a cloud, even the house of the LORD; So that the priests could not stand to minister by reason of the cloud: for the glory of the LORD had filled the house of God."

2 Kings 21:7 says, "...In this house, and in Jerusalem, which I have chosen out of all tribes of Israel, will I put my name for ever..."

In Ezekiel 48:35, God was assuring His people that His name and His presence would always be in Jerusalem. We see this fulfilled in Revelation 21:2-3:

"And I John saw the holy city, new Jerusalem, coming down from God out of heaven, prepared as a bride adorned for her husband. And I heard a great voice out of heaven saying, Behold, the tabernacle of God is with men, and he will dwell with them, and they shall be his people, and God himself shall be with them, and be their God."

As New Testament believers, we have the presence of God with us and in us.

"...and, lo, I am with you alway, even unto the end of the world. Amen" (Matthew 28:20).

"…for he hath said, I will never leave thee, nor forsake thee" (Hebrews 13:5:).

"Know ye not that ye are the temple of God, and that the Spirit of God dwelleth in you?" (1 Corinthians 3:16).

This is taken from two Old Testament scriptures:

> "And David said to Solomon his son, Be strong and of good courage, and do it: fear not, nor be dismayed: for the LORD God, even my God, will be with thee; he will not fail thee, nor forsake thee…" (1 Chronicles 28:20).

> "…as I was with Moses, so I will be with thee: I will not fail thee, nor forsake thee" (Joshua 1:5).

Therefore, we can celebrate the promise of Tabernacles as believers everyday since God is personally present with us – Jehovah Shammah. Wherever He is becomes our "there." Psalm 133:3 says:

> "As the dew of Hermon, and as the dew that descended upon the mountains of Zion: for there the LORD commanded the blessing, even life for evermore."

Ushpizin
Celebrating with Natural and Supernatural Visitors

The sages say "the only true joy is shared joy."

> "And thou shalt rejoice in thy feast, thou, and thy son, and thy daughter, and thy manservant, and thy maidservant, and the Levite, the stranger, and the fatherless, and the widow, that are within thy gates." (Deuteronomy 16:14).

It is a Jewish custom to recite what is known as the ushpizin (Aramaic for "guests") prayer inviting one of the seven shepherds of Israel. According to tradition, a different guest enters the sukkah each night followed by the others on successive nights. Each night readings are done from the teaching of that particular guest in agreement with the spiritual focus of that day. However, in some traditions, all visitors come each night.

The Bible teaches that when we eat and drink, we must also feed strangers, orphans, and widows. As each guest visits our sukkah, he empowers us with his particular anointing and enlightens us and our guests with his unique revelation of our Father. The supernatural guests are:

1. **Abraham** who embodies loving-kindness in Genesis 13:8-9, "And Abram said unto Lot, Let there be no strife, I pray thee, between me and thee, and between my herdmen and thy herdmen; for we be brethren. Is not the whole land before thee? separate thyself, I pray thee, from me: if thou wilt take the left hand, then I will go to the right; or if thou depart to the right hand, then I will go to the left."

   Jesus demonstrated loving-kindness to us in Mark 10:13-14, "And they brought young children to him, that he should touch them: and his disciples rebuked those that brought them. But when Jesus saw it, he was much displeased, and said unto them, Suffer the little children to come unto me, and forbid them not: for of such is the kingdom of God."

2. **Isaac** who portrays strength. Genesis 26:19-22, "And Isaac's servants digged in the valley, and found there a well of springing water. And the herdmen of Gerar did strive with Isaac's herdmen, saying, The water is ours: and he called the name of the well Esek; because they strove with him. And they digged another well, and strove for that also: and he called the name of it Sitnah. And he removed from thence, and digged another well; and for that they strove not: and he called the name of it Rehoboth; and he said, For now the LORD hath made room for us, and we shall be fruitful in the land."

   Jesus portrayed strength to us in John 18:4-6, "Jesus therefore, knowing all things that should come upon him, went forth, and said unto them, Whom seek ye? They answered him, Jesus of Nazareth. Jesus saith unto them, I am he. And Judas also, which betrayed him, stood with them. As soon then as he had said unto them, I am he, they went backward, and fell to the ground."

3. **Jacob** who represents truth. Genesis 32:24-28, "And Jacob was left alone; and there wrestled a man with him until the breaking of the day. And when he saw that he prevailed not against him, he touched the hollow of his thigh; and the hollow of Jacob's thigh was out of joint, as he wrestled with him. And he said, Let me go, for the day breaketh. And he said, I will not let thee go, except thou bless me. And he said unto him, What is thy name? And he said, Jacob. And he said, Thy name shall be called no more Jacob, but Israel: for as a prince hast thou power with God and with men, and hast prevailed."

   Jesus is the truth according to John 14:6, "Jesus saith unto him, I am the way, the truth, and the life: no man cometh unto the Father, but by me."

4. **Moses** who personifies the eternal word. Exodus 31:18, "And he gave unto Moses, when he had made an end of communing with him upon mount Sinai, two tables of testimony, tables of stone, written with the finger of God."

   Jesus is the living Word according to John 1:1, "In the beginning was the Word, and the Word was with God, and the Word was God."

5. **Aaron** who exemplifies divine splendor and majesty. Leviticus 16:2, "And the LORD said unto Moses, Speak unto Aaron thy brother, that he come not at all times into the holy place within the vail before the mercy seat, which is upon the ark; that he die not: for I will appear in the cloud upon the mercy seat."

   Jesus exemplified divine splendor and majesty in Matthew 17:1-2, "And after six days Jesus taketh Peter, James, and John his brother, and bringeth them up into an high mountain apart, And was transfigured before them: and his face did shine as the sun, and his raiment was white as the light." John 17:5, "And now, O Father, glorify thou me with thine own self with the glory which I had with thee before the world was."

6. **Joseph** who exhibits spiritual foundation and holiness. Genesis 39:7-10, "And it came to pass after these things, that his master's wife cast her eyes upon Joseph; and she said, Lie with me. But he refused, and said unto his master's wife, Behold, my master wotteth not what is with me in the house, and he hath committed all that he hath to my hand; There is none greater in this house than I; neither hath he kept back any thing from me but thee, because thou art his wife: how then can I do this great wickedness, and sin against God? And it came to pass, as she spake to Joseph day by day, that he hearkened not unto her, to lie by her, or to be with her."

Jesus exhibited spiritual foundation and holiness to us in Hebrews 4:15, "For we have not an high priest which cannot be touched with the feeling of our infirmities; but was in all points tempted like as we are, yet without sin."

7. **David** who symbolizes the establishment of the kingdom and sovereignty. 2 Samuel 7:11-13, 16, "And as since the time that I commanded judges to be over my people Israel, and have caused thee to rest from all thine enemies. Also the LORD telleth thee that he will make thee an house. And when thy days be fulfilled, and thou shalt sleep with thy fathers, I will set up thy seed after thee, which shall proceed out of thy bowels, and I will establish his kingdom. He shall build an house for my name, and I will stablish the throne of his kingdom for ever. And thine house and thy kingdom shall be established for ever before thee: thy throne shall be established for ever."

Jesus symbolized the establishment of His kingdom and sovereignty in Luke 1:30-33, "And the angel said unto her, Fear not, Mary: for thou hast found favour with God. And, behold, thou shalt conceive in thy womb, and bring forth a son, and shalt call his name JESUS. He shall be great, and shall be called the Son of the Highest: and the Lord God shall give unto him the throne of his father David: And he shall reign over the house of Jacob for ever; and of his kingdom there shall be no end."

May we embrace all of God's Word from both covenants everyday and experience a divine encounter. What a wonderful opportunity for evangelism we have in following the pattern of ushpizin. Inviting those we love to our homes and sharing the good news of the Gospel of Jesus Christ with them in the loving and unthreatening environment of our homes. Let's do it!

So Tabernacles is a time of remembrance, gratitude, and joy, but it is also a time of ingathering. In fact, one Hebrew name for this feast is *Chag Ha-asif* (khag hah-AH-siff) or "the Feast of Ingathering."

In the agriculture of Israel, Passover related to the planting season, Shavuot or Pentecost related to the grain harvest, and Sukkot or Tabernacles was identified with the fruit harvest.

This may explain the theme of joy more fully. Crops planted in spring don't bring their full "joy" until they reach their full maturity in the fall. So the harvesters' true rejoicing wouldn't come until the fall when all crops were harvested and the supplies were stored for the following year. Then the ultimate rejoicing for the ultimate harvest could begin!

Although the Feast of Tabernacles is about remembrance, it also has a prophetic meaning. The seven days of living in booths envisions *olam haba* (oh-lahm HAH-bah), the world to come, and the millennial reign of Jesus on earth when our Lord will "tabernacle" with us during His reign from Zion. This explains much of the theme of joy associated with this feast. God is near, dwelling with us, and both protecting us and providing for us in this world.

This explains why this feast is the only one that the Bible describes as being commanded for all nations. The Feast of Tabernacles is an acknowledgment of God's rule over the earth. To celebrate this feast is to affirm God's provident care and merciful governance of the world. All nations will have to come to this in time, or they will find themselves outside the blessing of God. Listen to the powerful words of Zechariah 14:16-19:

"The survivors from all the nations that have attacked Jerusalem will go up year after year to worship the King, the

LORD Almighty, and to celebrate the Festival of Tabernacles. If any of the peoples of the earth do not go up to Jerusalem to worship the King, the Lord Almighty, they will have no rain.

"If the Egyptian people do not go up and take part, they will have no rain. The LORD will bring on them the plague he inflicts on the nations that do not go up to celebrate the Festival of Tabernacles. This will be punishment of Egypt and the punishment of all the nations that do not go up to celebrate the Festival of Tabernacle" (NIV).

There is no mistaking God's requirement. He calls all nations to affirm that He is King of the universe and that He is their provider. He says that if any nation refuses to go up to Jerusalem and worship, it will have no rain – which means both literal rain and the things rain symbolizes: God's provision, abundance, rich harvests, and the blessings necessary for all of life.

This shows the power of the Feast of Tabernacles and God's feasts in general. They are part of the way we acknowledge God. They are conduits of His blessing. They are necessary not just for us as individuals or as churches but for the nations of the world. Ultimately, all nations will observe the feasts of God in Jerusalem, or they will be excluded, at least partially, from the blessing and protection of God. This moves the feasts from merely matters of historical memory and religious duty to the heart of what it means to submit to God's authority and rule.

Seven Days of Praise – The Lulav (loo-LAHV)

"And ye shall take you on the first day the boughs of goodly trees, branches of palm trees, and the boughs of thick trees, and willows of the brook; and ye shall rejoice before the LORD your God seven days" (Leviticus 23:40).

Traditionally this observance during Sukkot is known as the four kinds or species and also as the waving of the Lulav (Hebrew "palm branch"). Also known as *arba minim* in Hebrew or the *lulav* and *etrog*. During the seven days of Sukkot, the people were to rejoice before the Lord using four specific plants.

They were the etrog (citron fruit), the palm branch (lulav) which was by far the largest and most prominent, two willow branches (aravot) and three myrtle branches (hadassim). It is of interest to note that "myrtle" or Hadassah was Esther's Hebrew name, Esther 2:7:

> "And he brought up Hadassah, that is, Esther, his uncle's daughter: for she had neither father nor mother, and the maid was fair and beautiful; whom Mordecai, when her father and mother were dead, took for his own daughter."

The six branches were to be placed in a bundle in the right hand the citron fruit in the left to make a wave offering to the Lord. Each day the lulav was to be waved in six directions – north, south, east, west, above, and below declaring that God is surrounding and encompassing us in every direction. This certainly brings to mind, Psalm 91.

How comforting to know that our praise lifts up a shield of favor for us in every direction. Psalm 5:12, "For thou, LORD, wilt bless the righteous; with favour wilt thou compass him as with a shield."

The two major Jewish interpretations of the four kinds are first that they are symbolic of a body in harmony with all parts functioning in their respective places. Of course, as New Testament believers, we can immediately be drawn to the revelation of the body given by Apostle Paul in 1 Corinthians 12:12, "For as the body is one, and hath many members, and all the members of that one body, being many, are one body: so also is Christ."

Tradition teaches that the spine is represented by the long straight palm branch, the eye by the small oval myrtle leaf, the mouth by the long oval willow leaf, and the heart by the etrog fruit. These all can be used for sinful indulgences but should be used as members of righteousness. Romans 6:13:

> "Neither yield ye your members as instruments of unrighteousness unto sin: but yield yourselves unto God, as those that are alive from the dead, and your members as instruments of righteousness unto God."

The second leading interpretation of the lulav is that they are symbolic of the kinds of people that make up the Jewish people, or as New Testament believers we could easily see them as the church.

The sages say the etrog has both a taste and an aroma; so, too, do the people of Israel include individuals who have both Torah learning and good deeds. For New Testament believers, the church includes those who possess a knowledge of God's Word and who are doers of the Word also.

The date (the fruit of the lulav) has a taste but does not have an aroma; so, too, do the people of Israel include individuals who have Torah but do not have good deeds. For New Testament believers, the church includes those who possess a knowledge of God's Word but are not doers of the Word.

The hadas has an aroma but not a taste; so, too, do the people of Israel include individuals who have good deeds but do not have Torah. For New Testament believers, the church includes those are doers of God's Word but who do not who possess a knowledge of the Word.

The aravah has no taste and no aroma; so, too, do the people of Israel include individuals who do not have Torah and do not have good deeds... Says God: "Let them all bond together in one bundle and atone for each other."

For New Testament believers, the church includes those who possess neither a knowledge of God's Word nor are doers of the Word. There are those who have not yet accepted Christ as Lord and Savior, remember, they are yet children of God and I believe He will yet have them!

In Leviticus 23:40, while giving instructions for this festival, God commanded, "On the first day you are to take branches from luxuriant trees – from palms, willows and other leafy trees – and rejoice before the LORD your God for seven days" (NIV).

Thus, while the people of God construct their booths, they also assemble the branches for their lulav.

This takes the form of a long-stem bouquet used to decorate booths and wave before the Lord in dance and processions. We gain tremendous insight into the nature of our God through His prescriptions for His feasts.

Obviously, our King is generous, merciful, and kind. Yet He does not want His people to rely on their own sufficiency or to believe that they have prospered through their own efforts. Instead, He wants His people to celebrate His love for them. He wants them to dance, sing, shout, and declare, often using the very blessings that He has graciously provided. This is why He loves a wave offering of sheaves of grain on Firstfruits. This is why He wants loaves waved on Pentecost. And on the Feast of Tabernacles, He wants the branches of the vibrant trees of the land.

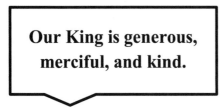

Our King is generous, merciful, and kind.

He has granted His people to be waved before Him and held aloft in gratitude. He does not ask this because He needs to be reminded of what He has done. He commands this in order to define the relationship He will have with His people. You see, the Feast of Tabernacles is not merely a religious regulation.

It is a call to a divine encounter with God. *Sukkot* also means "dwelling place." It can even mean "secret place," where the Almighty covers us with His wings. Where He overshadows us by presence and leaves us filled with His glory, with His power, and with the expectation of purposes yet untold. It is not just booths we are speaking of here. It is dwelling as one with the living God.

The Bible goes out of its way to let us know that Jesus celebrated Tabernacles when He walked the earth. One of the most revealing moments occurs in John 7. Jesus has gone to Jerusalem, and the Bible tells us that "halfway through the festival," He began to teach.

Opposition broke out, and there was such a stir that the chief priests and Pharisees sent men to arrest Jesus. Obviously, they were unable to lay a hand on Him, for the Bible tells us that on the last and greatest day of the festival, Jesus stood up and shouted in a loud voice words that would draw from the symbolism of the feast and echo through all time.

Before I recount His words, you should know that there was a ceremony observed during Tabernacles in which the high priest led a procession to the Pool of Siloam. This occurred on the seventh day of the feast, a special day called *Hoshana Rabbah* (hoe-SHAH-nah rah-BAH) or "The Great Salvation." The high priest filled a golden pitcher with water, returned to the courtyard of the Temple, and poured the water out on the people.

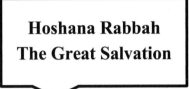

Hoshana Rabbah
The Great Salvation

Now, keep this ceremony in mind as you picture Jesus on this same day, shouting at the top of His voice in the same courtyard. Here is what He said:

"Let anyone who is thirsty come to me and drink. Whoever believes in me, as Scripture has said, rivers of living water will flow from within them" (John 7: 37-38, NIV).

Jesus was fearless, wasn't He? The high priest might have his golden pitcher filled with water from a local pool. Fine. This was the ritual, but the Living Christ declared before all men and for all time that He offered something far greater! To those who believed, He would give rivers of living water – and they would never cease as the water from the high priest's pitcher did.

The sages have said that "at the feast of Sukkot judgment is made concerning the waters." The amount of rain over the next few months after Rosh Hashanah would impact the next harvest. But hear our mighty King of Glory in Isaiah 12:3, "Therefore with joy shall ye draw water out of the wells of salvation."

And to the woman of Samaria in John 4:13-14, "Jesus answered and said unto her, Whosoever drinketh of this water shall thirst again: But whosoever drinketh of the water that I shall give him shall never thirst; but the water that I shall give him shall be in him a well of water springing up into everlasting life." And to you and me, Matthew 5:6, "Blessed are they which do hunger and thirst after righteousness: for they shall be filled."

For this has Messiah provided – Psalm 114:8, "Which turned the rock into a standing water, the flint into a fountain of waters."

Do you see that Tabernacles is a call to relationship? It is a call to power. It is a call to infilling with the Spirit of the living God. It is a call to dwell with the Holy One of Israel. No wonder Paul yearned for this cohabitation with God. No wonder he hungered for it and felt incomplete without it.

Remember his famous words in 2 Corinthians 5:2: "For in this we groan, earnestly desiring to be clothed with our habitation which is from heaven" (NIV). I might not even need to tell you that the "habitation" here is sukkot. Paul declared that no dwelling of this world will satisfy once we have experienced life in the sukkot of God. So we groan. Oh, how we groan, with yearning, until our dwelling from heaven is restored.

There is a beautiful and fascinating final feature of the Feast of Tabernacles. You remember that this feast is seven days long. Yet God requires an additional eighth day. We read of this in Numbers 29:35 where God said, "On the eighth day hold a closing special assembly and do no regular work" (NIV). Then God gave commands concerning the sacrifices to be made that day.

This eighth day is *Shemini Atzeret* (SHMEE-nee aht-ZEH-reht). *Atzeret* means to "abide, tarry or hold back." The wise rabbis through the centuries have concluded that it is as though God is asking those who have observed Sukkot to stay another day and "tarry" with Him. To remain. To stay with Him a while longer. The language of one ancient teaching moves me: "You may compare it to a king who had a festival for seven days and invited all the nations of the world to the seven days of feasting. When the seven days were over and the guests had gone, he said to his friend (Israel), 'Let us now have a small meal together, just you and I.'"[22]

How beautiful! How transforming! Our God calls us to His dwelling place, stirs us to worship Him in the intimacy of His blessing and presence, and then says, in essence, *Stay a while longer. I*

[22] Bamidbar Rabbah 21, Sukkah 55b.
Source: www.hope-of-israel.org/atzeret.html

love you. I would have you near another day. No wonder that Tabernacles is the final feast of the seven major feasts of God.

No wonder teachers and mystics through the years have viewed this festival as a sign of eternity. We would dwell with our God. He, in turn, would dwell with us and even bid us to tarry with Him forever in an eternity of celebration and fellowship when we will tabernacle with Him and He with us forever. Hear John shout it from Patmos in Revelation 21:3:

> "And I heard a great voice out of heaven saying, Behold, the tabernacle of God is with men, and he will dwell with them, and they shall be his people, and God himself shall be with them, and be their God."

A Final Thought

In Israel there is another celebration on Tishri 22, as well as *Shemini Atzeret, Simchat Torah* is also observed. However, outside of Israel (the diaspora), *Shemini Atzeret* is held on 22 and *Simchat Torah* on 23. Both immediately follow the seventh or last day of Sukkot but are not part of that feast.

Simchat Torah is defined as "rejoicing in the Torah" and marks the completion of the annual cycle of Torah reading which begins again immediately. This is symbolic that the Word of God is never ending and inexhaustible. Jesus says to us in Matthew 24:35, "Heaven and earth shall pass away, but my words shall not pass away." And Solomon reminds us wisely from Proverbs 4:20-22, "My son, attend to my words; incline thine ear unto my sayings."

ॐ ॐ ॐ

WISDOM OF THE RABBIS

The Greek grasped the present moment
and was the artist;
the Jew worshipped in timeless spirit
and was the prophet.
~ Isaac Mayer Wise

Chapter VII

JEWISH NEW YEAR...S?

"Now we look inside, and what we see is that anyone
united with the Messiah gets a fresh start, is created new.
The old life is gone; a new life burgeons [prospers]!"
(2 Corinthians 5:17, MSG).

It should come as no surprise to know that God looks at things differently from the way that men do. After all, He has a different perspective from His vantage point beyond the limitations of time and space. The ideas of time and space were created by God to enable His ultimate creation, man, to flourish and be fulfilled in a world God created especially for him.

As I mentioned earlier, God's way of measuring time from the fourth day of creation focused on the moon, which is a different way of perceiving time than the calendar that most of us in the Western world use, which is based on the sun.

God's appointed festivals always occur on the same day of the same month in the Jewish calendar, but those of us depending on the solar calendar wonder why Jewish holidays are in one month in a specific year and a different month in another year. Since the Jewish calendar is based on a lunar cycle that lasts 29.5 days, there are any number of discrepancies between God's appointed seasons and our more familiar calendar months.

However, since a month cannot include a half day, months on the Jewish calendar are either twenty-nine or thirty days. Lest you think this is confusing, just consider how difficult it is for most people to remember how many days are in a particular Gregorian month – it may be thirty, thirty-one, twenty-eight, or in leap years, twenty-nine.

In addition, focusing on the moon contributes to a different emphasis of the beginning of a day. When the description of creation was recorded in Genesis 1, the progression always moved from evening to morning to measure a day, whereas Western thinking tends to regard a day in terms of daylight (morning) to dark (night).

That is why according to the lunar calendar, special celebrations, including the Sabbath, always begin the evening before the calendar day. For Jews, a day begins at sundown and lasts until the following sundown. Keeping these principles in mind will help you understand much of the language of the Bible, especially when events in the Scriptures surround God's festivals.

When God spoke to His people about the specific times of year that He desired to meet with them for seasons of celebration, He instructed them to arrange these appointments according to the moon. That was the case when God intervened supernaturally to deliver His people from the oppression of slavery in Egypt:

"The LORD spake unto Moses and Aaron in the land of Egypt, saying, This month shall be unto you the beginning of months; it shall be the first month of the year to you" (Exodus 12:1-2).

Jewish months began with the new moon, which in ancient times was not what many Westerners think of as the "dark" phase of the moon, but the day the first sliver of the new, or waxing, moon appeared. This sliver of moon was reported and confirmed by Jewish authorities and was known as the head of the month. Today we have calendars based on calculations of the movements of the earth and the moon, but long ago the months were based on observation of the new moon.

When God gave Moses instructions for the Passover festival in Exodus 12, He specified that the month, or new moon, would be the first month of the year. The people of Israel were about to experience a rebirth as a result of their miraculous deliverance from their Egyptian taskmasters. They had new lives because of God's intervention, so it makes sense that they should consider this period of time the beginning of their year.

However, this understanding causes confusion when we see later that Rosh Hashanah, or the head of the year, is celebrated in the seventh month. Which is correct?

The short answer is that both are. Let me explain it this way. The first month, or Nisan, is the beginning of the sacred or ceremonial year and begins with the festival of Passover, which commemorates Israel's deliverance from Egypt. As we know from the biblical record, this was also the time that God chose to bring about the ultimate freedom from the bondage of sin, which culminated in the death, burial, and resurrection of Jesus.

The seventh month, or Tishrei, is the beginning of the civil year. It is the date from which years are counted for the purposes of Sabbath years and Jubilee years. It is also traditionally regarded as the date that began recorded history, which included the creation of Adam and Eve.

This discrepancy isn't so strange when we consider that many nations have different beginnings of years for different reasons. Many Western nations celebrate the beginning of a new year on January 1. This occasion involves revelry as well as a renewed determination to set goals, make resolutions, and manage affairs differently in the days to come.

However, for business and economic purposes governments and many corporations operate according to a fiscal year, which has entirely different beginning and ending dates. In addition, every parent of a school-age child is familiar with a school year, which usually begins in the fall and ends in the spring. You may actually celebrate more than one beginning of a new year without realizing that you're doing it.

Purim

Now allow me to take you to a feast that is not part of the original seven feasts of God and show you how we should make the *mo'edim* not a matter of history alone but a matter of experience in Jesus our Lord.

Our Jewish friends celebrate the feast of *Purim*. You won't find it commanded by God in your Bible, but you will find the story that gave rise to it. I want you to know its power and experience its blessing in your life. This feast of Purim takes place in the month of Adar, which is unique among all the months in the Hebrew calendar. Since the Hebrew calendar is a lunar calendar, the months are 29.5 days long. In other words, that's how long it takes to progress from a sliver-like crescent moon to a dark moon.

Just like the solar calendar we use, some time has to be made up every year. In the solar calendar, we call this a "leap year." One year in every four is longer than the rest. In the Hebrew calendar, this make-up time is accomplished within the month of Adar. Every so often, when it is needed, a year in the Hebrew calendar is called *shanah meuberet* (shah-NAH mee-oo-BEH-ret). It means "pregnant year." It is so named because this year is pregnant with an extra month, Adar 1.

So in the year that is pregnant – the year that is longer to make up the extra time created by the calendar – the month of Adar happens twice: Adar I and Adar II. This is why Adar is often called "the pregnant month." It has inside it another month that is born every so often when it is needed. Already, mysteries are revealed to us, and we haven't even gotten to the story behind Purim yet. Just the fact that Purim takes place in a pregnant month grants us revelation. We are instantly reminded that Jesus came in the "fullness of the time," according to Galatians 4:4 (NKJV). That means when the time was "pregnant." We are reminded that our God is a God who rules time and makes it serve His purposes. And He does this for our good.

> Our God is a God who rules time and makes it serve His purposes.

Our God can make the sun stop so that His people can win a battle. Our God can make time move backward so that the shadow on a sundial reverses itself. Our God can keep the shoes of His people from wearing out, meaning He can stop the ravages of time. Our God rules time, and He does it on our behalf.

You know what this means? It means our time is pregnant. It means that every hour we live is pregnant with meaning, with purpose, with even more time, and with God's multiplication.

Purim is a feast that celebrates the victory described in the book of Esther. You likely already know this story, but let me briefly review it.

In the Persian Empire there was a king named Xerxes. He was the son of Darius the Great. His queen was named Vashti, but she displeased her husband and he took as his wife instead a beautiful Jewish maiden named Hadassah or Esther. The king loved his new queen very much, but he did not know that Esther was Jewish, since she kept this a secret from him.

Esther had a cousin named Mordecai who was an advisor to her. Mordecai, a godly man, saw an evil man named Haman elevated to a high-ranking position by the king, but he would not bow to Haman. Haman was enraged by what he considered Mordecai's lack of respect for him, and he began plotting against all Jews. He convinced the king that the Jews were his enemies, and the king gave permission for Haman to do with the Jews as he pleased.

Esther's cousin Mordecai learned of Haman's intentions and reported them to her. Mordecai also told Esther that God had put her in her position "for such a time as this" (Esther 4:13, NKJV) so that she could deliver the Jews from the evil plots against them. It would mean, though, that Esther would have to tell the king she was Jewish. Doing that might cost her everything, even her life. She was a righteous woman, however, and concluded, "If I perish, I perish!" (Esther 4:16, NKJV).

Esther then arranged a banquet at which she intended to confront the evil Haman before the king. Before this banquet occurred, Haman had become so enraged with Mordecai – because he refused to bow to him – that he had a gallows built upon which he intended to hang Mordecai.

At her banquet, Esther told the king of the vast conspiracy that would take even her life. When the king demanded to know who had set the conspiracy into motion, Esther declared, "An adversary and enemy. This vile Haman!" (Esther 7:6, NIV).

Immediately, the king ordered Haman executed on the very gallows he had built for Mordecai. Then the king gave Queen Esther the estates once owned by Haman. He appointed Mordecai to a high office in the empire, and Esther convinced her husband, the king, to spare the Jews and to issue an edict on their behalf.

Soon afterward, the Jews arose against all their enemies. People of other nationalities helped them, and they triumphed completely. It was such a moment of victory that Mordecai instructed all the Jewish people to celebrate the feast of Purim to honor God for the deliverance He wrought for His people. The date of this Purim would be the fourteenth of Adar – the pregnant month – and the people would observe it for all time.

This is the glorious story of the victory that God brought about through a young Jewish woman named Esther. It is a thrilling story, and we ought to remember its lessons forever. Yet my purpose in recounting it is to show you that the themes of this story and this feast are fulfilled for you in Jesus. In other words, Jesus is saying to you even in Purim, "This scripture is fulfilled in your hearing."

Let me tell you that for those who serve Jesus, there is going to be a hanging. Because Jesus is your defender, because He loves you and watches over you, and because His glory is your rear guard, He will destroy those who oppose you.

The very ones who conspire against you and build gallows to end your life will find that God is able to confuse their plans and destroy them with the very weapons they would have used on you. There's going to be a hanging! It will be a hanging of the ones who have intended to hang you.

And why? Because God is for you. Because God intends good for you. Because He has adopted you and made you His own. Because what He did for Esther He will do for you. Yes, there is going to be a hanging! A hanging of every enemy arrayed against you.

So in a time pregnant with purpose and in a time of deadly threat, God's servant is positioned to play a role, is inspired by an anointed voice to act courageously, and ends up bringing deliverance to you at just the right moment.

I'm not talking about Esther. I'm talking about *you*. *You* are chosen. *You* are positioned. *You* are given anointed counsel, and *you* have the capacity for courageous action that delivers those of your generation. This is all true because of what Jesus has done in your life.

Your time is pregnant. Your life is pregnant. And there is a power in you able to do more than all you can ask or imagine.

Do you see how the meaning of Purim grants us revelation that is fulfilled right now in Jesus Christ? It is the same with all the feasts of God. They are *mo'edim* – sacred signs revealed in sacred times with God for fulfilling sacred purposes.

May the Lord fulfill His every feast and sign in you!

Epilogue

THESE WORDS ARE FULFILLED

In these pages we have surveyed the feasts of the living God. We have reminded ourselves of their history, pondered the magnificence of their ceremonies, and taken hold of their meaning for all who are in Christ. I am not finished yet. I want to seal all that we have seen in your heart by taking some of Jesus' most powerful words and helping you see them through the lens of a feast we have not examined yet.

In Luke 4:14, we read of a moment early in Jesus's earthly ministry in which He is returning to His hometown in Galilee. He has been baptized by John. He has conquered temptation in the wilderness. Now, He is going to the city of His childhood: Nazareth.

As was His custom, He went into the synagogue on the Sabbath, and as He entered, He was given the scroll of the prophet Isaiah to read. He chose these words:

"The Spirit of the Lord is on me, because he has anointed me

to proclaim good news to the poor. He has sent me to proclaim freedom for the prisoners and recovery of sight for the blind, to set the oppressed free, to proclaim the acceptable year of the Lord's favor" (Luke 4:18-19, NIV).

These are the words of Isaiah 61:1-2, and they describe the "year of the Lord's favor." Their immediate application is to the Year of Jubilee, the fiftieth year when all debts were canceled, all slaves were freed, rest was commanded, and God's blessing was proven more than sufficient to sustain His people. Yet the broader application of these words was to the messianic age, as the rabbis wrote. It was to the ultimate millennial rule of the Messiah.

Now, focus on this single moment. Jesus has read the words of an ancient prophecy in the synagogue of Nazareth. These beloved words have been read in that place many times before. Faithful men and women memorized them and longed for the Jubilee – which, if they were fortunate, might happen once in their lives – and for the ultimate rule of the Messiah on earth.

Keep watching Jesus. He stands to read this famous passage and then sits down. This is the position of one who will teach the verses just read. All eyes are on Jesus as His eyes sweep over the eager crowd.

Then He says it: "Today this scripture is fulfilled in your hearing" (Luke 4:21, NIV). They are among the most powerful words He would ever speak on earth. In fact, they may be the banner over His entire earthly life. He was saying, *What you have been waiting for, what you have longed for the Messiah of God to do one day, can be done right now and right here. I am that Messiah. You must wait no longer, not for fifty-year cycles or the return of the Messiah. I am He. All that is promised is possible at this moment.*

Though His audience would not fully understand it, every healing, every deliverance from poverty, every recovery of sight, every victory over oppression needed in that place was possible. Jesus was among them. Their Jubilee ceased to be a date or an age. Jesus was their Jubilee. The time had come. Nothing more was needed.

I remind you of this dramatic moment in Jesus's life because I want you to know that this is the way it is with all God's feasts and all God's promises. They are all "yes," and they are all "right now" in Jesus. The time has come because He has declared it. The time has come because He holds time in His hands. There is nothing symbolized, promised, or anticipated in any of the feasts we have studied that you must wait to experience. Jesus is that fulfillment, and He is with you now.

We do not have to wait for a given day of the year to experience the liberation of Pesach or Passover. Jesus is that liberation. We do not need to wait for fifty days after Firstfruits so that once a year we can experience abundance. Jesus is that abundance. How urgent it is that you grasp this truth. Jesus is the fulfillment of all and the answer to all. We keep the feasts to understand what He has done and what He will do. The doing, though, is in Jesus right now.

It is as true now as it was on that day in Nazareth: "Today this scripture is fulfilled in your hearing."

Appendix

THE JEHOVAH NAMES OF GOD

The Bible tells us in no uncertain terms that the name of God carries earth-shattering power. His name conveys His glory. His name conveys His character. His name conveys His irresistible strength. To draw close to God and to know Him intimately, it is important to learn His names. Our English words for God do not carry the detail and nuance that the Hebrew names for God do. We should learn these Hebrew names and use them as we pray, worship, and declare His will on earth as it is being done in heaven.

Make it your goal to memorize as many of these names as you can. Meditate on them. Use them often. Most of all, allow them to paint a more accurate and transforming picture of who God is on your heart. Doing this will set you on the course of a deeply God-centered life. and it will help you view God through a more biblically Hebraic lens.

Jehovah – the Lord *(Exodus 6:2-3)*
Adonai Jehovah – the Lord God *(Genesis 15:2)*
Jehovah Adon Kal Ha'arets – Lord of All the Earth *(Joshua 3:11)*
Jehovah Bara – the Lord Creator *(Isaiah 40:28)*
Jehovah Chezeq – the Lord My Strength *(Psalm 18:1)*
Jehovah Chereb – the Lord the Sword *(Deuteronomy 33:29)*
Jehovah Eli – the Lord My God *(Psalm 18:2)*
Jehovah Elyon – the Lord Most High *(Genesis 14:18)*
Jehovah 'EzoLami – the Lord My Strength *(Psalm 28:7)*
Jehovah Gador Milchamah – the Lord Mighty in Battle *(Psalm 24:8)*
Jehovah Ganan – the Lord Our Defense *(Psalm 89:18)*
Jehovah Go'el – the Lord Thy Redeemer *(Isaiah 49:26; 60:16)*
Jehovah Hashopet – the Lord the Judge *(Judges 11:27)*
Jehovah Hoshe'ah – the Lord Saves *(Psalm 20:9)*
Jehovah 'Immeku – the Lord Is with You *(Judges 6:12)*
Jehovah 'Izoz Hakaboth – the Lord Strong and Mighty *(Psalm 24:8)*
Jehovah Jireh – the Lord Will Provide *(Genesis 22:14)*
Jehovah Kabodhi – the Lord My Glory *(Psalm 3:3)*

Jehovah Kanna – the Lord Whose Name Is Jealous *(Exodus 34:14)*

Jehovah KerenoYish'I – the Lord the Horn of My Salvation *(Psa. 18:2)*

Jehovah Machsi – the Lord My Refuge *(Psalm 91:9)*

Jehovah Magen – the Lord the Shield *(Deuteronomy 33:29)*

Jehovah Ma'oz – the Lord My Fortress *(Jeremiah 16:19)*

Jehovah Hamelech – the Lord the King *(Psalm 98:6)*

Jehovah Melech 'Olam – the Lord King Forever *(Psalm 10:16)*

Jehovah Mephalti – the Lord My Deliverer *(Psalm 18:2)*

Jehovah M'gaddishcem – the Lord Our Sanctifier *(Exodus 31:13)*

Jehovah Misqabbi – the Lord My High Tower *(Psalm 18:2)*

Jehovah Naheh – the Lord that Smiteth *(Ezekiel 7:9)*

Jehovah Nissi – the Lord Our Banner *(Exodus 17:15)*

Jehovah 'Ori – the Lord My Light *(Psalm 27:1)*

Jehovah Perazin – the Lord Is Thy Breakthrough *(2 Samuel 5:20)*

Jehovah Rapha – the Lord that Healeth *(Exodus 15:26)*

Jehovah Rohi – the Lord My Shepherd *(Psalm 23:1)*

Jehovah Saboath – the Lord of Hosts *(1 Samuel 1:3)*

Jehovah Sel'I – the Lord My Rock *(Psalm 18:2)*

Jehovah Shalom – the Lord Our Peace *(Judges 6:24)*

Jehovah Shammah – the Lord Is There *(Ezekiel 48:35)*

Jehovah Tsidkenu – the Lord Our Righteousness *(Jeremiah 23:6)*

Jehovah Tsori – the Lord My Strength *(Psalm 19:14)*

Jehovah 'Uzam – the Lord Their Strength *(Psalm 37:39)*

Jehovah Yasha – the Lord Thy Savior *(Isaiah 49:26; 60:16)*

A GLOSSARY OF HEBREW TERMS

Counting of the Omer: The counting of the days between Passover and Shavuot, announced daily during Passover along with a blessing; intended to remind Jews of the link between Passover, which commemorates the Exodus, and Shavuot, which commemorates the giving of the Torah.

Days of Awe: The name for the ten days from Rosh Hashanah to Yom Kippur, a time for introspection and consideration of the sins of the previous year.

Feast of Firstfruits: This feast celebrates the first yield of the harvest in spring. It is comprised primarily of a wave offering of a sheaf of grain by a priest. There followed the sacrifice of a male lamb. This celebration reminded God's people of His provision for their every need.

Feast of Passover (or *Pesach* [PAY-sahk]): The first of three pilgrimage festivals with historical and agricultural significance. This feast commemorates the Jewish Exodus from Egypt in which God "passed over" the houses of the Jews that bore the blood of the sacrificial lamb on their doorposts.

Feast of Tabernacles (or Booths or *Sukkot* [soo-KOTE]): This is the third of three pilgrimage festivals with historical and agricultural significance. This feast commemorates the gathering of the harvest and God's provision for the people of Israel in their wilderness wanderings. Traditionally, Jews live in booths for one week to recall their deliverance from Egypt and subsequent wilderness journeys.

Feast of Weeks (or Pentecost or *Shavuot* [sha-voo-OHT]): This is the second of three pilgrimage festivals with historical and agricultural significance. This holiday commemorates the giving of the Torah at Mount Sinai and celebrates the spring harvest.

Hoshana Rabbah (hoe-SHAH-nah rah-BAH): Also known as the last of the Days of Judgment, which began on Rosh Hashanah, this is the seventh day of the Feast of Sukkot on which seven circuits are made around the synagogue reciting a prayer with the refrain, "Hoshana!" meaning, "Please save us!"

Hyssop: The biblical use of this word refers to one of several herbs that have aromatic and cleansing properties, grow wild in Israel, and can easily be bunched together to be used for sprinkling in instances of religious purification. This hyssop was used to apply the blood of sacrificial animals.

Jubilee: Coming at the end of seven cycles of sabbatical years, the Year of Jubilee—the fiftieth year—was one in which slaves were freed, debts were forgiven, and both land and people were granted rest.

Kosher: Food that is permissible to eat under Jewish dietary laws. This term can also describe any other ritual object that is fit for use according to Jewish law.

Lulav (loo-LAHV): A collection of palm, citron, myrtle, and willow branches used to fulfill the commandment to "rejoice before the Lord" during the Festival of Sukkot.

Moed, plural Mo'edim (moh-EHD; moh-eh-DEEM): A Hebrew term that refers primarily to the five "festive seasons" of God. It means "festivals and set or appointed times" as well as to "signify" or "act as a sign."

Pesach Sheni (PAY-sahk- SHAY-nee): A "Second Passover" for anyone who was unable to bring the offering on its appointed time. This occurs every year on 14 Iyar, exactly one month after 14 Nisan, which is the day before Passover.

Purim (poo-REEM): A Jewish holiday commemorating the deliverance of the Jewish people in the ancient Persian Empire. This deliverance is described in the book of Esther.

Rabbi: A religious teacher authorized to make decisions on issues of Jewish law. The term literally means "My Master."

Rosh Hashanah (or Feast of Trumpets [rahsh hah-SHAH-nah]): Literally the "head of the year," Rosh Hashanah marks the Jewish New Year. It is the first of the Fall Feasts that begin in the seventh month. It was marked by resting, blowing trumpets, having a holy convocation, and making offerings by fire to the Lord.

Sage: A person of profound wisdom. *Sages* refers generally to the greatest Jewish minds of all times. Sometimes also referred to as Chazal, which is an acronym of the Hebrew phrase "Chachameinu Zichronam Liv'racha," meaning "our sages of blessed memory." In its strictest sense, *Chazal* refers to the final opinions expressed in the Talmud but is sometimes used more loosely to refer to the generally accepted opinion of any of the wise people who have contributed to Jewish law.

Shemini Atzeret (SHMEE-nee aht-ZEH-reht): Meaning "Eighth Day of Assembly," this holiday is distinct from, yet connected to, the Festival of Sukkot and serves as an opportunity for the Jewish people to spend extra time with God after Sukkot.

Shemittah (SHMIH-tah): The seventh year of the seven-year agricultural cycle mandated by the Torah and still observed in contemporary Judaism. During Shemmitah, the land is left to lie fallow, and all agricultural activity, including plowing, planting, pruning and harvesting, is forbidden.

Shofar (show-FAHR): A ram's horn, blown like a trumpet usually as a summons to the people. Shofars are used in Scripture to summon God's people to repentance, war, worship, and rest.

Siddur (see-DOOR): A Jewish prayer book, containing a set order of daily prayers.

Simchat Torah (SEEM-kaht TOH-rah): Concurrent with Shemini Atzeret and meaning "Rejoicing in the Torah," this holiday marks the completion of the annual cycle of weekly Torah readings.

Talmud (TAL-mood): The collection of Jewish law and tradition consisting of the Mishnah and the Gemara and being either the edition produced in Palestine a.d. c400 or the larger, more important one produced in Babylonia a.d. c500.

Tetrad: A series of four consecutive total lunar eclipses occurring at approximately six-month intervals.

Torah (TOH-rah): Meaning "Instruction" or "Teaching." In its narrowest sense, the Torah is the first five books of the Bible: Genesis, Exodus, Leviticus, Numbers, and Deuteronomy, sometimes called the Pentateuch or the Five Books of Moses. In its broadest sense, the Torah is the entirety of Jewish teachings, written and oral.

Trumpets: Often *shofars* (ram horns), trumpets are used for summoning the congregation, for sounding an alarm, for going to war, and in worshipping God. See also: *Rosh Hashanah.*

Unleavened Bread: Also known as *matzo*, this bread without yeast is served during Passover, the festival celebrating the Exodus from Egypt. The Israelites left Egypt in such haste they could not wait for their bread dough to rise; the bread, when baked, was *matzo*. *Matzo* also symbolizes redemption and freedom, while serving as a reminder to be humble and not forget what life was like in servitude.

Yom Kippur (or Day of Atonement [yohm kee-POOR]): A day set aside for fasting, depriving oneself of pleasures, and repenting from the sins between men and God during the previous year. Yom Kippur occurs on the tenth day of Tishrei and completes the annual period known as the Yamim Nora'im *(*Days of Awe) that commences with *Rosh Hashanah.*

WORDS FROM HEBREW CEREMONIES

❧   ❧   ❧

The Passover Seder

The Jewish observance of Passover (the Hebrew word is *Pesach*) centers on a Seder meal that includes readings from the Torah, object lessons, words from ancient rabbis, and even ritual questions asked by children. This ceremonial meal is defined in the *Haggadah*, "the telling," which is named in fulfillment of the charge in Exodus 13:8 that parents tell their children the story of God's preservation when death and the curse "passed over" the children of Israel in Egypt: "Thou shalt shew thy son in that day, saying, This is done because of that which the LORD did unto me when I came forth out of Egypt."

The Blessings and Prayers

The Passover Seder includes the following opening blessing:

Blessed are You, God, our God, King of the universe, who has chosen us from among all people, and raised us above all tongues, and made us holy through His commandments. And You, God, our God, have given us in love a holy convocation, commemorating the departure from Egypt. For You have chosen us and sanctified us from all the nations, and You have given us as a heritage Your holy Shabbat and Festivals in love and favor, in happiness and joy. Blessed are You, God, who sanctifies the Shabbat and Israel and the festive seasons.

During this Seder, four cups of wine are consumed, each commemorating one of four promises from Exodus 6:6-7:

"Say unto the children of Israel, I am the LORD, and I will bring you out from under the burdens of the Egyptians, and I will rid you out of their bondage, and I will redeem you with a stretched out arm, and with great judgments: And I will take you to me for a people, and I will be to you a God: and ye shall know that I am the LORD your God, which bringeth you out from under the burdens of the Egyptians."

1. I will bring you out (the Cup of Consecration)
2. I will free you (the Cup of Deliverance).
3. I will redeem you (the Cup of Redemption).
4. I will take you as my own people
   (the Cup of Restoration or Praise).

Remember that Jesus was performing this Seder meal with His disciples when He took the third cup of wine, the Cup of Redemption:

> "He took the cup, and gave thanks, and gave it to them, saying, Drink ye all of it; For this is my blood of the new testament, which is shed for many for the remission of sins" (Matthew 26:27-28).

Among the many words from Scripture read during the Seder meal are these joyous words that recall the return of Israel from captivity in Babylon:

> "When the LORD turned again the captivity of Zion, we were like them that dream. Then was our mouth filled with laughter, and our tongue with singing: then said they among the heathen, The LORD hath done great things for them.

> "The Lord hath done great things for us; whereof we are glad. Turn again our captivity, O LORD, as the streams in the south. They that sow in tears shall reap in joy. He that goeth forth and weepeth, bearing precious seed, shall doubtless come again with rejoicing, bringing his sheaves with him" (Psalm 126).

At the end of the Seder, this traditional prayer is spoken:

> *Blessed are You, Lord our God, King of the universe for the vine and the fruit of the vine, for the produce of the field, and for the precious, good and spacious land which You have favored to give as an heritage to our fathers, to eat of its fruit and be satiated by its goodness. Have mercy, Lord our God, on Israel Your people, on Jerusalem Your city, on Zion the abode of Your glory, on Your altar and on Your Temple. Rebuild Jerusalem, the holy city, speedily in our days, and bring us up into it, and make us rejoice in it, and we will bless You in holiness and purity and remember us for good*

on this day of the Festival of Matzo. For You, Lord, are good and do good to all, and we thank You for the land and for the fruit of the vine. Blessed are You, Lord, for the land and for the fruit of the vine.

Finally, there is the traditional chant, "Next year in Jerusalem!"

The Texts

The texts read during Passover include the following:

Exodus 12:1-4: The Passover Lamb
Leviticus 23:5: The date for Passover
Numbers 9:1-14; 28:16: Rules for the observance of Passover
Deuteronomy 16:1-7: The description of unleavened bread

◈ ◈ ◈

The Feast of Unleavened Bread

The Feast of Unleavened Bread, or *Chag HaMatzoht*, is part of Passover. Specifically the focus is on the eating of unleavened bread as a remembrance of the original Passover night.

The Blessings and Prayers

Because Passover and the Festival of Unleavened Bread are observed together as parts of a whole, the Chag HaMatzoht blessings and prayers would be included in the Passover services above.

The Texts

The texts read during Chag HaMatzoht include the following:

Exodus 12:21-51: The story of Passover
Numbers 28:16-25: Rules for the observance of Passover
Joshua 3:5-7, 5:2-6:1, 6:27: Passover in Canaan

◈ ◈ ◈

The Feast of Firstfruits

The Feast of Firstfruits, or *Reshit Katzir* (reh-Sheet kaht-ZEER), occurs the day after the Sabbath included in the Feast of Unleavened Bread.

The Blessings and Prayers

Reshit Katzir is part of Passover and is included in the Passover services described above. In addition, the priests bless the congregation with the priestly blessing during the Musaf prayer, which is the additional prayer service said during some holy days.

The Texts

The texts read during the Feast of Firstfruits include the following:

Exodus 33:12–34:26: Covenant promises to Israel
Numbers 28:19-25: Rules for the seven days of Reshit Katzir
2 Samuel 22:1-51: David's song of deliverance

∼ ∼ ∼

The Feast of Weeks

The Feast of Weeks, or *Shavuot*, occurs fifty days after Pesach and commemorates the giving of the Torah and the harvest of the firstfruits. The rabbis teach that the reason Shavuot is not on a particular date, but instead is marked by the counting from Passover, is to keep the remembrance of Passover always in the forefront.

Because the festival is a celebration of the giving of the Torah, it is traditional to stay up all night reading Scripture on the evening before the first day and then begin the first day of Shavuot with prayer. The holiday is marked by using decorations of greenery and eating dairy and sweets (milk and honey). Every evening includes a festive holiday meal.

The Blessings and Prayers

As the sun sets on the eve of Shavuot, candles are lit and this blessing is said:

Blessed are you, God, Our God, Sovereign of the Universe, who has made us holy with commandments and has commanded us to light the festival candles.

And blessed you are, God, Our God, Sovereign of the Universe who has let us live and sustained us and has brought us to this time.

137

A special holiday Kiddush (sanctification) is spoken before each meal:

Praised are You, Adonai our God, Ruler of the world, who creates the fruit of the vine.

And then:

Praised are You, Adonai our God, Ruler of the world, who brings forth bread from the earth.

The Texts

The texts read during Shavuot include the following:

Exodus 19-20: The giving of Torah to the Israelites
Leviticus 23:15-21; Deuteronomy 16:9-12, 16-17: The specific rules for Shavuot
The book of Ruth: Included perhaps because it was during the spring harvest that Ruth was gleaning in the field of Boaz. Ruth became the grandmother of King David and therefore is an ancestor of Jesus.

༚ ༚ ༚

The Feast of Trumpets

Rosh Hashanah, which occurs in the fall on the first and second days of the Hebrew month of Tishrei, is one of the Jewish nation's holiest festivals and celebrates the creation of the world. Interestingly, the name "Rosh Hashanah" is not used in the Bible, but instead the holiday is called Yom Ha-Zikkaron (the day of remembrance) or Yom Teruah (the day of the sounding of the shofar), and is instituted in Leviticus 23:24.

The holiday is filled with deep meaning and is the subject of thousands of pages of written text. Just a few aspects of the observance of Rosh Hashanah are acknowledging the sovereignty of God, spending time in contemplation and personal renewal, and offering prayers for the year to come. Jews around the world celebrate in many ways, including wearing new clothes, attending synagogue, and listening to the shofar (ram's horn) being blown.

Regular daily liturgy is expanded for Rosh Hashanah, and a special prayer book called the *machzor* is used for Rosh Hashanah and

Yom Kippur because of the extensive liturgical changes required. A few of the special segments are below.

The Blessings and Prayers

We praise You, Eternal God, Sovereign of the Universe, who makes us holy with mitzvot and commands us to kindle the lights (of the Sabbath) and of the Day of Remembrance

Shehecheyanu: Who Has Kept Us Alive

Blessed are you, Lord, our God, sovereign of the universe Who has kept us alive, sustained us, and enabled us to reach this season.

Special Additional Segments to the Rosh Hashanah Service:

Hamelech: Acknowledging God as Sovereign
Avinu Malkeinu: Acknowledging God as our Father and King
Musaf for Rosh Hashanah: Prayer with three extra sections
Malchuyot: Again focused on the sovereignty of God
Zichronot: Remembrance, both God's remembrance of His covenants with His people, and the worshipper's remembrance of promises made
Shofrot: The Power of the Shofar

The Texts

The texts read during Rosh Hashanah include the following:

Genesis 1: The creation of the world.
Genesis 21: The story of the miraculous birth of Isaac and God's promise to Sarah.
1 Samuel: The answer to Hannah's prayer, the birth of a son, Samuel.
Genesis 22: Abraham's willingness to sacrifice his son, Isaac.
Jeremiah 31: God's everlasting love for His people and the future ingathering of Israel's exiles.

૮ૐ   ૮ૐ   ૮ૐ

Yom Kippur

Yom Kippur, which occurs in the fall on the tenth day of the Hebrew month of Tishrei, is the most important holiday of the Jewish calendar. It commemorates the day when God forgave His people for creating and worshipping the golden calf. Yom Kippur, commanded in Leviticus 23:36, is the time set aside to atone for the sins of the past year. On Yom Kippur, the book that holds the record of those sins is sealed; therefore any chance to change that judgment by amending wrongs or repenting of sins ends at the close of the holiday.

Yom Kippur includes a complete fast of food and water, and for Orthodox Jews, even washing, using cosmetics and deodorants, and wearing leather clothing are prohibited. Traditionally, white clothing is worn, and the holiday is spent primarily in the synagogue for morning, afternoon, and evening services, which end with the sounding of the shofar.

The all-day services include far-reaching prayers of confession and supplication, including a prayer to annul unwise vows, confession of the sins of the community, and petitions for forgiveness – most of which involve repentance for the mistreatment of others.

The Blessings and Prayers

Kol Nidrei, more a proclamation than a prayer, this is spoken three times, from soft to loud:

All vows we are likely to make, all oaths and pledges we are likely to take between this Yom Kippur and the next Yom Kippur, we publicly renounce. Let them all be relinquished and abandoned, null and void, neither firm nor established. Let our vows, pledges and oaths be considered neither vows nor pledges nor oaths.

May all the people of Israel be forgiven, including all the strangers who live in their midst, for all the people are in fault.

O pardon the iniquities of this people, according to Thy abundant mercy, just as Thou forgave this people ever since they left Egypt.

The Lord said, 'I pardon them according to your words.

Shehecheyanu Who Has Kept Us Alive

Blessed are you, Lord, our God, sovereign of the universe

Who has kept us alive, sustained us, and enabled us to reach this season.

The Texts

The texts read during Yom Kippur include the following:

Leviticus 16:1-34: Description of the service performed by the high priest, the role of the scapegoat, and the atonement of sins for the Israelites.

Leviticus 18:1-30: Commandments against perverse sexual practices.

Isaiah 57:14-58:14: Assurance of God's forgiveness and comfort, and admonishment for a righteous fast and true observance of the Sabbath.

Book of Jonah: Jonah's rebellion, time spent in the belly of a whale, repentance, and mission.

Micah 7:18-20: God's delight in showing mercy.

❧ ❧ ❧

The Feast of Tabernacles

The Feast of Tabernacles, or *Sukkot*, is a weeklong fall celebration commemorating the Israelites' forty-year wandering in the wilderness. During this festival, Jews build and dwell in temporary shelters, imitating their ancestors' journey.

The Blessings and Prayers

SUKKOT KIDDUSH: Kiddush is recited while holding a cup of wine or other liquid, no less than 3.3 ounces.

Blessed are you, Lord, our God, sovereign of the universe
Who creates the fruit of the vine (Amen)
Who made all things exist through His word (Amen)

Blessed are you, Lord, our God, sovereign of the universe
who has chosen us from among all people, and exalted us above
every tongue and sanctified us with His commandments, and you
gave us, Lord our God, with love appointed festivals for glad-
ness, festivals and times for joy this day of the festival of Sukkot,
the time of our gladness
a holy convocation, a memorial of the exodus from Egypt
because you have chosen us and made us holy from all peoples
and your holy festivals in gladness and in joy you have given
us for an inheritance
Blessed are you, Lord, who sanctifies Israel and the season.

THE BLESSING FOR DWELLING IN THE SUKKAH: This blessing should be recited at any time you are fulfilling the mitzvah of dwelling in the sukkah, for example, before you eat a meal in the sukkah.

Blessed are you, Lord, our God, sovereign of the universe
Who has sanctified us with His commandments and com-
manded us to dwell in the sukkah.

SHEHECHEYANU Who Has Kept Us Alive

Blessed are you, Lord, our God, sovereign of the universe
Who has kept us alive, sustained us, and enabled us to reach
this season.

Drink the Kiddush wine after the Shehecheyanu blessing.

FAREWELL TO THE SUKKAH: This farewell blessing refers to the "hide of the Leviathan," because traditional Jewish teaching says that the giant sea creature will be slain when Messiah comes, and its hide used as a sukkah.

May it be Your will, Lord, our God and God of our ancestors
that just as I have stood up and dwelled in this sukkah so
may I merit next year to dwell in the sukkah of the hide of
the Leviathan.

Next year in Jerusalem!

The Texts

The texts read during Sukkot include the following:

Leviticus 22:26-23:44: The specific rules for Sukkot and other holidays.
Numbers 29:12-16: Other rules, and the description of the Temple offerings for Sukkot.
Zachariah 14:1-21: A description of the end times.
Kings 8:2-21: The dedication of Solomon's temple.

[More information about all of the feasts and the liturgies of the feasts can be found at Chabad.org.]

Have you made *heaven* your eternal home?

If not, there's no better time than right now, and a caring *Breakthrough* prayer partner is ready to minister to you in prayer when you call our toll free *Breakthrough Prayer Line*, **(888) 534-3838**. They'll also send you a copy of Pastor Rod Parsley's booklet, *New Direction* that will help you along your walk with the Lord.

24 hour live stream of anointed messages and powerful music!

Dedicated **iPastors** are available online to pray with you and support you. Chat **LIVE** during service times, or email your needs as you watch the anointed programming on our 24/7 stream of worship and ministry from World Harvest Church.